PRAISE FOR RES

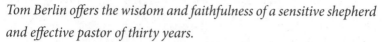

Tom Berlin offers the wisdom and faithfulness of a sensitive shepherd and effective pastor of thirty years.

> -**The Reverend Canon Jan Naylor Cope**, Provost,
> Washington National Cathedral

Through these captivating yet provocative pages, Berlin is at his best: thoroughly biblical, deeply pastoral, profoundly theological, and passionately missional.

> -**Sathianathan Clarke**, Bishop Sundo Kim Chair for
> World Christianity; Professor of Theology, Culture
> and Mission, Wesley Theological Seminary

Tom Berlin's book is a treasure of insightful discussions that focuses on the "messes" in peoples' lives and how we can be restored and transformed. I found it to be a great source of inspiration.

> -**Sharma D. Lewis**, Bishop,
> Virginia Conference, The United Methodist Church

In Berlin's capable hands, a dog with a mouth full of couch cushion, a poll on stink bugs, and an "intrusive" vine in a neighbor's yard all become occasions for exploring the gap we create between ourselves and a God who is always reaching out to love us.

> -**Ginger E. Gaines-Cirelli**, Senior Pastor,
> Foundry United Methodist Church, Washington DC

Pastor Tom Berlin has written this book through the eyes of his heart. I could see the handiwork of God in every chapter.

> -**Brenda Girton-Mitchell**, Inductee, Martin Luther King Jr.
> College of Preachers, Morehouse College

TOM BERLIN

RESTORED

FINDING REDEMPTION
IN OUR MESS

Abingdon Press / Nashville

RESTORED

Finding Redemption in Our Mess

This book is printed on elemental chlorine-free paper.

Library of Congress Cataloging-in-Publication data applied for.

978-1-5018-2292-6

16 17 18 19 20 21 22 23 24 25—10 9 8 7 6 5 4 3 2 1

MANUFACTURED IN THE UNITED STATES OF AMERICA

To my daughters, Rebekah, Kathryn, Hannah, and Sarah.
Children help fathers understand both their mess
and their need for redemption through the love of Christ.
You have done it with grace.
What you find here is what I know to be true.

Finally, brothers and sisters, rejoice! Strive for full restoration, encourage one another, be of one mind, live in peace. And the God of love and peace will be with you.

(2 Corinthians 13:11 NIV)

CONTENTS

INTRODUCTION

I am a pastor. In my job, I work with people who are trying to figure out how faith in Christ can guide and direct their lives. I've done this for about thirty years, and I've gotten to know many of these people pretty well. Some have entrusted me with their stories. When you are a pastor, you never know when people are going to tell you their stories. It can happen at dinner, in a hallway, or in a van on the way to a mission trip. Twice I've seen an airplane seat turn into a confessional booth. The five minutes when a someone drops by my office can become a much longer discussion of burdens the person finally has decided to share. Stories are a big deal. Hearing the story of someone's life is a sacred trust. When people are really honest with you, it's always an experience of holy ground.

Having heard so many stories over the years, here is what I can tell you: people are a mess. Don't take that the wrong way. It's true of me, too. It's not that everyone's life is falling apart all the time;

it's simply that we all have some mess in our lives. Sometimes we have a lot of mess, the accumulated junk of a lifetime.

We have stuff that others have said or done to us, which often produces shame that we carry around for years. Conversely, things we have said and done to others have generated chaos, leaving us with guilt. We know we should not have done that bad junk, but there we go again. Shame and guilt are bullies. They push us around and tell us we are unworthy, unlovable, and unredeemable. They are the kind of things that people sometimes approach pastors to talk about. People want to know if anyone has insight into what's going on in their lives.

Pastors turn to the Bible to shed light on what is going on in our messes. One thing I love about the Bible is its honesty. It's not a book full of shiny-happy people whose deep obedience to God and disdain for temptation prevent the problems faced by the rest of us. If you have some mess in your life, have no fear; people in the Bible are almost always standing in something deeper. If God had the patience to work with them, you can be sure that the Almighty will be present for you, too.

This book arose from people's stories and our conversations. In the book, I try to order the ideas that resulted and to share some of the insights that Scripture offers us. The chapters began as sermons in a series that I preached during the weeks of Lent. I love the season of Lent. In those days before Easter, Christians are willing to do hard work. Pastors encourage their flocks to hunker down and take a hard look at their lives.

During the sermon series, I found that talking with the congregation about our collective mess produced an unusual level of honesty that was free of judgment and claims of superiority.

People understood that all of us struggle with similar issues. Those attending worship came with a desire to hear how God's grace could help them experience transformation. Church members in small groups encouraged each other to attend to a life in Christ.

Those experiences were especially meaningful during Lent, but they can occur any time of year. Whenever people commit to do spiritual work together, we can hear Christ knock at our doors. He wants to help us see ourselves clearly and begin to put things right. Doing it together in a churchwide series with small-group study turned out to be uniquely effective in our congregation. It created conversations in families and among friends that people found helpful and healing. However, this book was written so that anyone anywhere could experience restoration through Christ.

I've called the book *Restored* because restoration is the goal of the Christian life. Honesty about our mess is important, but it can also be depressing unless we remind ourselves of the ultimate goal. The good news of the gospel is that by the grace of Christ, found in the love and power of his death and resurrection, we can be restored to the image of God in which we were created.

The mess is obvious. God's grace is the greater part of our story. Grace is subtle and seeking. It is the means that God uses to transform our narrative. Our continued response to the work of grace is what leads to our restoration.

We were created in God's image, but for many of us, sin has made that a distant memory. In this book we will walk together through the process of redemption, from mess management to life restoration. In each chapter, I will use theological terms that may be helpful. You will hear about grace in all its forms: prevenient grace, justifying grace, and sanctifying grace. If that last sentence makes little sense, have no fear; I will explain and discuss each term and how it has meaning for our lives. You will also hear about the importance of Christ's death and resurrection, and how Christ makes us at one with God. Spiritual disciplines and practices that will help us stay connected with God will be shared, because many people start the Christian journey only to lose energy over time. You will see that the process of restoration will not only help us personally; it will equip us to share good news with others.

Finally, we will see that not only can God enable you to change and clean up your mess, but you can be fully transformed, learning to love God and others the way Jesus did. That may sound hard to believe, but it is God's goal for your life. The Lord doesn't want to settle for less. Christ wants you to be more of the person you were created to be.

I hope that this book and the related materials will be a blessing, enabling you to find hope in the love that God holds for you. Though you may quickly resonate with the idea that all of us are a bit of a mess, I hope you will become deeply convinced that all of us, by the grace of God, can have the abundant life that Christ offers.

1

THIS IS A REAL MESS

The desire to do good is inside of me, but I can't do it. I don't do the good that I want to do, but I do the evil that I don't want to do.

(Romans 7:18-19)

Sometimes the thing you're searching for appears right in front of your face. That's how I felt when thinking about how to start this book. I was looking for a way to talk about the distance between God and us, and the reason that so many of us find that in one way or another, or many ways at once, we are a mess.

This was on my mind as I attended a three-day denominational meeting. Above the stage, a giant logo was projected onto the screen, showing a detail of Michelangelo's famous work *The Creation of Adam*, which was painted on the Sistine Chapel ceiling.

The image consists of two hands. The one on the right is the hand of God, reaching toward Adam, trying to make contact and infuse him with life. The hand on the left belongs to Adam, who reaches feebly back, fingers slack, as if thinking: *I don't know. I kind of maybe want what God is offering. Sort of. Not sure. I hope to get around to it. I need to think about it awhile.*

For three days I contemplated those two hands and was reminded how perfectly they portray the human condition. Though the fingers, hands, and arms gained my attention, I found the most interesting part of the picture to be the gap between God's finger and Adam's. It was the tiniest of gaps, but there was a Grand Canyon of distance within it.

What is represented in that gap? It is the *almost* of life—what we would have, and could be, if only we would reach toward God as energetically as God reaches toward us. That gap is the distance between the life we have and the life we want. It is the empty space in the relationship with God that we feel even as we long for full communion with the one who created us.

Michelangelo's work is based on Genesis 1:26:

> *Then God said, "Let us make humanity in our image to resemble us so that they may take charge of the fish of the sea, the birds in the sky, the livestock, all the earth, and all the crawling things on earth."*

Art historian Paul Barolsky points out that Michelangelo departed from the depiction of God at creation offered by other artists of his time. They typically placed God either hovering above the earth at a great distance or standing on earth while creating humans and animals. Michelangelo did something far more dramatic and biblical. He showed God soaring toward Adam. When you stand in the Sistine Chapel and look at the piece, your eye will inevitably compare the figure of God in active pursuit to the figure of Adam in passive repose. Other than posture, the two are all but identical and give new meaning to the phrase, "Let us make humanity in our image."[1]

At the same time, the artist brought to life another creation passage, Genesis 2:7:

> The LORD God formed the human from the topsoil of the fertile land and blew life's breath into his nostrils. The human came to life.

Michelangelo depicted the moment when God imparted life and spirit to Adam. Here the *imago Dei,* the image of God, is completed.

Created in the Image of God

The Bible says we have been created in the image of God. Think about the implications of that for a moment. If you are in a place where there are other people, look around and see what they look like. If you can get to a mirror, hold it up and take yourself in for a moment. The Spirit of the Creator graces your countenance. It is in the face of the person next to you.

You knew this when you were a child. There has always been a part of you that you knew deserved some level of recognition by others. As an infant, when an adult seemed kind, you put your arms out so the person could pick you up and admire you more closely. When another kid in preschool was interested in the way you played with the construction toys on the playground, it made sense that she wanted to join you. At lunch in elementary school, when a boy paused near your table, as if he hoped for an invitation to sit down, you could see why. In those days you were comfortable with the fact that people liked to interact with you.

Likewise, as you grew older the opposite experiences hurt for the same reason. When you learned that a group of friends all went to the movies and didn't invite you, it stung. When you asked the girl for a date and she replied, "No, thanks," it didn't matter how nicely she said it; you experienced it as a denial of something good inside you. When your parents didn't notice how many hours you invested to make that B- in chemistry, it was disappointing. You wondered if it would always require the best mark before they would recognize the good that came from you.

This feeling of worth that you possess is not about you. It is not that you feel superior to others. What is happening in those moments is an unconscious realization that God is in you. Let me be clear. You are not God. But you were made by God. You were made in the image of God. The goodness of the Creator is stamped deep inside your being. That is your identity, and it can be your reference point. That is what theologians mean when they speak of being created in the *imago Dei*.

However, we have a problem. We often don't see the goodness of God that is right before our face, or in our face, as the case may be. And we often don't see it in each other.

My friend Erin told me of an embarrassing moment she had while walking her dog. In one garage that she passed, a couple was openly arguing. It was a heated exchange. They were inside the garage, but the door was up, so they could be seen and heard plainly. Because three walls surrounded them, they apparently felt as though no one else could hear them. Erin knew it was socially appropriate to keep looking forward and walk briskly past. Unfortunately her small terrier did not understand social conventions. He was fascinated by the sight of two humans exchanging verbal volleys. He went to the end of his leash. He paused and stared. His head moved back and forth, following the action. Erin gave him a gentle tug. He sat down. The dog was entranced by the way the people were treating each other. The man and woman continued their verbal sparring. Erin tugged again. The dog was going nowhere. She finally had to walk over, pick up the dog, and walk away. The couple in the garage never paused.

People can be a real mess. By "people" I mean me, you, and everybody else. We lose sight of the beauty God has placed in our own lives and the lives of others. Consider for a moment how many people you know who are doing great in every way. I'll bet there aren't many. Even those who appear to be fine from the outside are often dealing with inner difficulties.

> People can be a real mess.
> We lose sight of the beauty God
> has placed in our own lives and
> the lives of others.

Some difficulties are beyond our influence. We don't control cancer. We can't stop the flash flood that ruins our home. But most hardships are of our own making. He has maxed-out credit cards and unmanageable interest payments because of unchecked spending. She runs late all the time and compensates by driving too fast, and now if she gets one more ticket her license will be suspended and she will have no way to get to work. Many of us have unresolved issues in our past and habits we seem unable to give up, even though the negative impact is tangible.

This is the mess I am talking about. Think about your life. Now think about the people you love and care for. How many of them have a mess of some sort in their lives right now?

During an interview, actor Bill Murray was asked about being a bachelor. He had been married twice and was currently not in a relationship. Murray said it would be nice to have a female companion for wedding receptions or great trips. He added, "But there's a lot that I am not doing that I need to do.... I don't have a problem connecting with people. My [issue] is connecting with myself...."

Then Murray shared a great insight into what keeps people from doing the deeper work of looking at their lives candidly:

> What stops [any of] us is we're kind of really ugly
> if we look really hard. We're not who we think we
> are. We're not as wonderful as we think we are. It's
> a little bit of a shock.... It's hard.[2]

When Bill Murray says that we're really kind of ugly, he is not talking about the image of God in which we were created. He's talking about something else. Theologians have a word for it. In plain English, it's called sin.

Looking at Sin

Sin is a word that people don't use as much as they once did. This is too bad, because it explains a lot of human behavior.

When I say *sin*, what comes to mind? You may think of individual moral failures, such as anger, abuse, assault, or adultery. That's four, and I haven't even exhausted the *A*'s! Imagine if we walked through the alphabet. We may be safe at *Z*, but that's about it. Sin can also happen on a social scale, such as when a company allows effluent from its factory to despoil a nearby river, or when a society makes people live in a certain place because of their race. Sin also includes sins of omission, such as when someone drives past a motorist on the side of the road who is in obvious distress.

Any of these would be good examples of a sin. The ugliness that we see when we look hard at our lives, however, is something much broader. We don't struggle with a particular sin. We suffer from the condition of sin. We live in a state of sin, and it holds us captive and prevents us from experiencing the life that we could enjoy.

Think of sin as an illness that affects the condition of every human. This is often called *original sin*. Unfortunately, when people think of original sin they often go to the original humans, Adam and Eve, and wonder if one bite of an apple could really do so much generational harm. It seems silly to think that one act of disobedience set the entire human race off course. The issue, however, is far greater than a bite of apple. It is the state of willful disobedience against the good, just, and beautiful order that our Creator attempts to bring to our world and lives. The disobedience of Adam and Eve is similar to decisions all of us make. It is original in the sense that it is foundational. The problem is common to us all.

The Hebrew language has multiple words that can be translated into English as *sin*. I think one of the most descriptive is *pasha*, which means "to rebel" or "to revolt." Have you ever felt that you were rebelling against something but did not know what it was or why it was important to you? Have you ever felt drawn to something you knew was wrong and would eventually lead to harm but did it anyway?

We have been created in God's image, but we revolt against it. Think of the couple in the garage. Even a dog could see that it was not God's will for them to exchange harsh words in their supposed privacy, much less in front of their neighbors. Maybe that's why the terrier was so fascinated. In some ways we could say this same thing about any sin in our lives or the lives of others: clearly it is not God's will.

What's interesting is that often it's easy to see sin in the lives of others but hard to detect sin in our own. The problem is that our souls are sick. The condition of sin is the illness. The particular sin committed in a given moment is just a symptom of the deeper condition. As with a bad cough, just because you make it stop for a moment doesn't necessarily mean you are cured of the infection.

Not only is the soul sick; it has been sick for so long that we have grown accustomed to it. As a result, it's often easier to notice the health of righteousness than the illness of sin. That's why you feel so good when you help an elderly person pick up a bag of spilled groceries, but you may not feel bad or even notice when you yell at a guy who's driving too slow on a crowded freeway.

You can tell when you are dealing with the condition of sin in your life. Boundaries feel oppressive and ridiculous. You read the

Bible and find its advice to be passé; obviously the Good Book simply does not understand your very special circumstances. A friend gently quotes a verse as a reminder, and you find yourself angry or hurt. This is the thinking that occurs when you have a big gap between you and God.

When the image of God is closer to the surface of your personality, the wisdom of the Bible reflects what you believe is true and good in the world and offers a protection from harm.

When the image of God is closer to the surface of your personality, the wisdom of the Bible reflects what you believe is true and good in the world and offers a protection from harm. Many years ago, my wife Karen and I were hiking in a national park out west. The trail took us down by a large creek that led to a river. We knew that the water was cold and fast-moving, but the sound drew us to the edge. There we found a sign with the words *Stay back! If you fall in, you will die.*

We did not question that sign. We did not think someone put it there to limit us or rob us of fun. We assumed it had been put there out of concern for our safety, and because of it we completed the journey we had begun with great memories. The difference between those two ways of thinking about the wisdom of the sign is an indicator of emotional, mental, and spiritual health. When we are experiencing the condition of sin at a full fever, there is no reasoning with us. When we are thinking clearly, we gain great perspective on the good intentions God has for us.

Think of sin as a thick film in your being that covers the image of God. I visited the Sistine Chapel recently and was surprised to find that the place looked new, even though it was centuries old. I learned that only a few years earlier it had undergone a full restoration. Through the centuries, the art in the Sistine Chapel had been affected by numerous elements including candle smoke, incense, pollution, dust, humidity, and the visitors who walk through daily. The stain caused by all those elements had muted the colors and details of Michelangelo's artistry.

On the Vatican grounds you will find exhibits that show the impact of the recent restoration. "Before" and "after" photographs demonstrate how clouded with grime and soot the paintings had become. With each frame you can see the work of the restoration process, first removing the grime coating and then restoring the color of the original work. Though the restoration project was not without controversy, its effect enables one to imagine the splendor of the day in the 1500s when people first beheld Michelangelo's work and the joy they must have found in its unveiling.

There are two things that I believe to be true about you and me: (1) We were created in God's image. This means we are greater masterpieces than the art Michelangelo left on the ceiling of the Sistine Chapel. (2) The grime of sin covers us and hides the great beauty God intended for us and the world to enjoy.

Some of us struggle to believe the first point. People sometimes convince us that we are of little worth, or we have experiences in life that harm us deeply, and as a result we can no longer sense our own beauty.

The second point, however, can be equally difficult to accept about ourselves. In fact, most of us either don't believe we need to change a whole lot or don't want to devote a great deal of energy to the effort. This may be why the word *sin* isn't used with as great a frequency as it was in the past. At our worst, we can often describe the changes others need to make and feel superior to them for sins they commit.

At a family gathering, two of the youngest members, girls who were about five at the time, were jumping on the couch together. One child's mother told them to stop before they hurt themselves or the couch. The girls did as they were told and played on the floor for a few minutes. Then they got back up on the couch and began bouncing again. As they were jumping, one child called to her mother, "Mommy, look at what she is doing!"

Ever noticed how easy it is to see the sins of others, and how difficult it is to accept that you have the same problem? But if you embrace the idea that there is a film of sin covering the masterpiece of God's image that is embossed on your being, it is possible to be open to a full restoration of what has been damaged. Through the grace of God and the work of Christ, you can be healed of what ails you. The Apostle Paul spoke of restoration when encouraging the church in Corinth:

> *Finally, brothers and sisters, rejoice! Strive for full restoration, encourage one another, be of one mind, live in peace. And the God of love and peace will be with you.*

(2 Corinthians 13:11 NIV)

The God of love and peace will indeed need to be with us if the image of God is to be restored in us. But it can happen. That may be why Jesus is often referred to as the Great Physician. He healed many with a variety of physical ailments. He is able to do the same for those who suffer from the various maladies of sin. However, we have to participate in our own healing.

The Pharisee and the Tax Collector

Jesus told a parable about two men who were very different in the way they dealt with their ugly insides. One man was a Pharisee, the other a tax collector. Jesus' audience was struggling with the same issues you and I deal with every day.

> *Jesus told this parable to certain people who had convinced themselves that they were righteous and who looked on everyone else with disgust.*
>
> (Luke 18:9)

The Pharisees were a religious sect of Judaism, begun in the second century B.C., that focused its attention on keeping God's law and doing exactly what God asked, down to the details. If there was a lack of clarity in the Scripture, they added new rules to make sure they did not cross any unhealthy boundaries.

Now, the pursuit of righteousness is a good thing, but sin can ruin even the best of intentions. By the time of Jesus, the Pharisees had become so oriented to the rules that they could be condemning, self-righteous, and unaware of their own sin sickness. We can see this in the parable Jesus told:

> *Two people went up to the temple to pray. One was a Pharisee and the other a tax collector. The Pharisee stood and prayed about himself with these words, "God, I thank you that I'm not like everyone*

> *else—crooks, evildoers, adulterers—or even like*
> *this tax collector. I fast twice a week. I give a tenth*
> *of everything I receive."*

(Luke 18:10-12)

Note several things about the Pharisee in Jesus' parable. He prays about himself but not for himself. It's as if he has come to the temple to remind God of his goodness rather than to glorify the goodness of God. He prays in the normal fashion of that day, with his head up to God, while attitudinally he looks down on the sinners around him. Rather than honoring God with his fast and tithe, the Pharisee ends his prayer with the implication that God should honor him because of his fast and tithe.

By contrast, we have the tax collector. Jewish tax collectors for Rome were considered to be terrible people. They were complicit with the Roman oppression of Israel. Paid very little by the Roman government, they were allowed to bully and extort their own neighbors for money. They were sometimes brutal and willing to extract money from the most vulnerable people in their town or village. A Jewish tax collector with any remaining conscience would never be comfortable near the temple. The tax collector in Jesus' parable has something going on in his life or he wouldn't be there. Pangs of regret have made their way into his psyche. A fresh wind is blowing.

> *But the tax collector stood at a distance. He wouldn't*
> *even lift his eyes to look toward heaven. Rather, he*
> *struck his chest and said, "God, show mercy to me,*
> *a sinner."*

(Luke 18:13)

Pay attention to the tax collector and you will see the beginning of a restoration project. Notice that he stood at a distance from the temple where Jews believed God resided. He knew he was far from God, and he was humbled by his sin. He prayed for himself and expressed no judgment of those around him. His prayer contained not a word of comparison with others. This tax collector, taking on an unusual posture for prayer at that time, looked to the ground and beat his chest in mourning over the condition of his life. This tax collector was a lot closer to God than anyone could imagine.

Jesus made this observation: "I tell you, this person went down to his home justified rather than the Pharisee" (Luke 18:14a).

The word *justified* is important if you want to understand God's work of restoration. The justification icons on any word processing program are like magic. Highlight a paragraph, click the button, and suddenly all the text lines up on the left, right, or center. To fully justify means that the text falls evenly against both the right and left margins of the page.

If you work with wood, you know how hard it is to open a door that's out of alignment with the frame, or to deal with the problems that come when boards warp and go askew. The wood has to be justified to be useful. The door frame may need to be deconstructed and reassembled; the boards might need to be worked with a plane or sander.

To be justified is to be aligned to the proper standard, to be brought into conformity with others so that one can be of use. To be justified before God, we must first realize that we are out of alignment.

That is why Jesus pointed to the tax collector and said that he was justified that day at the temple. The tax collector did not win the contest for most eloquent prayer. He did have the deepest insight about the condition of his own life and the sickness of his soul. The tax collector was justified before God, because admission of a bad life is the first step in finding a new life. You have to deal with the grime before you uncover the masterpiece.

Jesus used the example of a tax collector so we would know he was talking about a very bad man. But notice that God did not give the tax collector what he deserved as a reprehensible person; instead, God offered a surprising grace. The man was justified. He was given God's love and God's power for change.

If the first step toward justification is realizing we are out of alignment, the second step is getting honest about who we are and accepting that the Master Artist has not given up on us. Unless we believe that God can see the beauty hidden beneath our sins, hang-ups, and mess, we will never be able to accept the Lord's forgiveness and restoration.

> Unless we believe that God can see the beauty hidden beneath our sins, hang-ups, and mess, we will never be able to accept the Lord's forgiveness and restoration.

By contrast, the Pharisee left the same way he had arrived, probably feeling a deeper sense of self-righteousness because he could check the box that said "prayed today." Beware encounters with God that do not leave you with a sense of humility or gratitude for God's grace. Rather than praying, "My life is a mess," the Pharisee was saying, "Don't mess with me." When that happens, it's a sign that we are not fully giving ourselves over to God. Nothing hinders God's work of restoration like an outer coating of pride.

Jesus ended his parable with a powerful observation: "All who lift themselves up will be brought low, and those who make themselves low will be lifted up" (Luke 18:14b).

Facing our condition of sin is one of the most important things we can do in life. If we embrace the fact that we suffer from this universal illness, we won't need to be anxious at the thought that we have sinned or deny the existence of sin in our lives. We will give up believing that we are better than others and become empathetic to the ways sin manifests itself in their lives. Being free of anxiety about sin will allow us to consider how we might change and restore the fullness of God's image within us.

I understand the Pharisee's reluctance to get real. Who wants to come before God or a friend or a group of strangers and say, "I have some mess in my life"? But it's the very thing that will open us to healing.

Stop Trying to Manage Your Sin

If we can own our sin, we can get rid of our old strategies for sin management. Here are two strategies that people commonly pursue.

Denial

Most of us know how to project our best self and deny the rest, first to ourselves and then to others. We look good as much as possible, but when someone raises a concern about our behavior or words, we deny the problem. Like a magician covering a sleight of hand, we must give people something else to look at so they don't see what is right before them. We might say, "I have my issues, but they aren't as bad as the ones of people I read about in the news—professional athletes being arrested, politicians being charged, violent people threatening our society."

Here's my personal favorite: "I may have done that, but why is everyone so upset? It's not like I'm an ax murderer!"

I want to say, "Congratulations, you're not an ax murderer! Well done, sir. I have a certificate of appreciation here somewhere. Now, about your drinking problem.... "

Denial is a fear-based reaction. We fear that people will not love us if they know who we are, so we deny what is obvious to everyone. In doing so, we show we don't understand that God extends true love and grace not because of who we are but despite who we are. Fear drives us to portray an image of perfection that serves as a smokescreen so no one will see who we really are, and it leaves us feeling lonely.

Admiring the Problem

Some people spend a lifetime saying, "This is just who I am. You have to accept it." Others want to help them and offer support or strategies for change, but these people never seem to do more than talk about their issues and the impact their decisions have had over the years. In this strategy's worst form, people who admire the problem become apathetic and spiritually listless. They are stuck. Some will give up believing in God altogether. If God does not exist, there is no path to transformation. It becomes easier to make a home in the abyss than find a path home.

This strategy may be a consequence of the shame we experience when we get honest about our sin. Most people, when they see the impact their sin has had on others, feel embarrassed. This can lead to low self-esteem that denies the image of God in which we were created. When looking at ourselves, we should behold something like Vincent van Gogh's beautiful *Starry Night*, but instead we see *Dogs Playing Poker*.

Philo of Alexandria was a Jewish philosopher who lived in Egypt at the time of Christ. One saying attributed to him is "Be kind, for everyone you meet is waging a great battle."

The great battle is the conflict we feel between the goodness of God's image within us and the sin that so often controls us. There is a masterpiece down there, but it has been covered with a thick veneer of gunk as our condition of sin has led to our habits of sin. The humility Jesus calls us to experience grants plenty of room for compassion to others and an equal amount of patience with ourselves.

You may be a mess. You may be stuck. But there is hope. You can recognize your need to bridge the gap between you and God, and you can understand that you are powerless to do so on your own. You may not be aware of it, but right now God is on the move. Right now, God is reaching out to you.

2

WHO LEFT THIS MESS?

You are saved by God's grace because of your faith. This
salvation is God's gift. It's not something you possessed.
It's not something you did that you can be proud of.

(Ephesians 2:8-9)

The presence of a puppy in our house meant that we had
given up.

Don't get me wrong—we like dogs. We had enjoyed our dog
Woody for many years before his death. Because of Woody's
advanced age and our daughter Sarah's youth, she had never really
experienced an active dog.

My wife Karen and I knew we did not want another dog. We
gave many good reasons not to get a dog. But Sarah, our fourth
daughter, who now lived alone with her aging parents, had rebuttal

arguments that would rattle any prosecuting attorney. She was persistent as a mosquito, returning even after we successfully swatted back her repeated requests.

I'm not sure when or how it happened, but one day Karen and I just broke. A puppy born to a foster dog on St. Patrick's Day would be coming to live with us in six weeks. By the time you get to the fourth child, you are a weakened version of your former self.

It wasn't long before we came to love the little puppy with the very large paws. Sarah named him Mudge, after the dog in the Henry and Mudge books. The real dog and fictional dog had similar markings and personality. Mudge quickly grew from a bouncing puppy to an eighty-five–pound muscle with legs. In the first year he did all the predictable things a puppy will do. We were patient. We hired a puppy trainer and delighted in his ability to sit, stay, and come ... under controlled circumstances. We knew he would grow up, and with age and continued training would come better impulse control.

Mudge made real progress by his first birthday. He could be left alone in a room without supervision. He was better behaved on walks. We had determined that when we were gone, he could be left uncrated in a gated area of our house, and he rose to the occasion. At just a little over a year, we felt Mudge had left his puppy ways behind and had matured into the well-behaved dog we knew he could be.

In early June both Karen and I needed to be away, so one of our older daughters came to stay with Sarah and Mudge. The girls started off with the best of intentions, but their days were full of activities and obligations, so Mudge did not receive the amount of attention to which he was accustomed. Days passed. The bone and chew toy we had left him with became smaller and smaller, and less and less interesting. Perhaps some walks were skipped. Whether overcome with anxiety or just simple curiosity, something happened to Mudge on Day 6 of this temporary-care arrangement.

By Sunday I had been gone a week. I was ready to relax. I had missed Mudge and was looking forward to seeing him. As I opened the front door, I could hear something in the next room. I was surprised Mudge did not run to greet me and assumed that he was in his crate.

When I turned the corner into the living room, I stopped in my tracks. Debris was everywhere. I picked up a piece and realized it was foam padding. There was cotton padding as well, everywhere. It covered the floor of the living room. Mudge was in the middle of the room, a large piece of foam in his mouth and a look that said, *I'm not sure what came over me, but this is so much fun! You can still get in on it if you like!*

At first I couldn't figure out the source of all that foam and cotton. Then I looked at the couch. There was a big hole where the center cushion had once been. I looked at the couch, then at Mudge, back at the couch, and back at Mudge. For a moment I didn't know what to do. Then I pulled out my smartphone and said, "Mudge! You sit!" It must have been my tone of voice, as Mudge's delight quickly faded and he sat immediately. I took a photo of Mudge and his mess to share with Karen.

To this day, Karen and I laugh when we see that photo. The wreckage of the room makes it obvious that Mudge had lost himself in the thrill of it all. Simply by entering the room I had made him aware of the mess he had made. The look on his face says that he knows it was wrong to bring such wanton destruction to the couch cushion. He may be a dog, but he is not ignorant of his sin. His expression carries the distinct look of guilt. His ears are out and flat. His head is slightly extended. Karen and I looked up these features on the Internet and learned that in dog language, Mudge was showing us he was "anxious and ashamed." Mudge had made a mess, because Mudge was a mess.

Messes Come in Many Forms

I've seen that same look on a lot of human faces over the years, including my own. You may know what I'm talking about. You find yourself in a mess of your own making. It was satisfying while it lasted, but when you pause and survey the damage, you wonder, *Who left this mess?* The issue isn't just who is at fault; it's a question of motivation. Why do we do the things we do? How do we get in situations that are so difficult to undo?

A man is standing in his bathrobe in the hallway, looking out the small window next to his front door. His wife left for work a few minutes ago. The kids spent the night at a friend's house. It is January. The ground outside is covered with a recent snow. The driveway is shoveled bare, with patches of ice. On the thin, cleared strip of the sidewalk, he can see his newspaper. The temperature is about ten degrees above zero. He is barefoot but feels daring. He decides to go for it. He opens the door and steps out onto the landing. Halfway to the newspaper, he feels a gust of wind and hears the door close with an ominous "click."

He is in a mess.

Messes happen all the time to all sorts of people. Most messes have far more impact than figuring out how to get back into a house when the front door is locked. Messes can be destructive.

Have you ever noticed that when you find yourself in a mess, you wonder how you got there? It's sort of a surprise. One day she has a particularly bad argument with her husband that ends in anger and tears. He used to be her best friend, but now they argue all the time. As she walks away, she thinks, *How did we get here?*

He feels low on energy and creaky when he walks. He ran track in high school and was in great shape when he was in the Army. Now he looks in a mirror and sees more of himself than he can ever remember. He realizes that he hasn't eaten right, exercised, or even taken a vitamin for a very long time. He wonders, *How did this happen?*

She sends out another resume, hoping for an interview. She was recently let go from her third job in two years. She just can't seem to get along with those she describes as her demanding supervisor and petty co-workers. Her performance appraisals contain adjectives about her work and personality that make her angry. She doesn't believe them. Now the slow job search makes her worry about finances. She thinks, *Why is this happening to me?*

Messes come in many forms, and all of them have a backstory. One of the most common reasons for the mess in our lives has to do with our posture toward God. We lean in the wrong direction.

People often have a posture problem. We are leaning away from God at the exact moment when we should lean in.

A Posture Problem

When you examine Michelangelo's *The Creation of Adam*, notice that while God is using every ounce of the divine being to make contact, Adam's body creates space between them. Adam is reclined, and the curve of his form suggests that he makes no effort to meet the Lord halfway. Adam is relaxed and appears both apathetic and disinterested.

People often have a posture problem. We are leaning away from God at the exact moment when we should lean in. While God is reaching for us, we are examining our options. There are so many things to do in life besides doing God's will or living God's ways.

In his Letter to the Galatians, the Apostle Paul talks about two different ways of living. The first way is to be led by the Spirit. The second way is to do life on our own terms and to live from one encounter to another guided by our emotions, our desires, and the priorities we create on our own. Paul warns that the second way does not lead to a good outcome, when he writes:

> *I say be guided by the Spirit and you won't carry out your selfish desires. A person's selfish desires are set against the Spirit, and the Spirit is set against one's selfish desires. They are opposed to each other, so you shouldn't do whatever you want to do. But if you are being led by the Spirit, you aren't under the Law. The actions that are produced by selfish motives are obvious, since they include sexual immorality, moral corruption, doing whatever feels good, idolatry, drug use and casting spells, hate, fighting, obsession, losing your temper, competitive opposition, conflict, selfishness, group rivalry, jealousy, drunkenness, partying, and other things*

> *like that. I warn you as I have already warned you,*
> *that those who do these kinds of things won't inherit*
> *God's kingdom.*

(Galatians 5:16-21)

Read that over once more, but this time consider how much of the mess humans create in their lives is described here in six short verses. Think about your life and the lives of people you know personally and people you see in the news. How many of their messes arise from sexual immorality or misconduct, the failure to live by good morals or ethics, unrestrained pursuit of a good time, drug and alcohol abuse, conflict that includes fighting, stalking, anger mismanagement, a desire for conflict, distrust, group rivalry, and selfishness? Paul captures the majority of the mess of our lives in a very succinct passage.

If you make a list of the messes in your life right now, or in the lives of those you love such as children, siblings, friends, and co-workers, you will find that nearly everyone's issues are in one of the categories Paul provides. But again, the problem is not the particular sin. It is the condition of sin. It is a posture problem. We are leaning away from God at the moment when God is trying to reach us.

Paul wants us to know that another life is available to us.

> *But the fruit of the Spirit is love, joy, peace, patience,*
> *kindness, goodness, faithfulness, gentleness, and*
> *self-control. There is no law against things like this.*
> *Those who belong to Christ Jesus have crucified the*
> *self with its passions and its desires.*

(Galatians 5:22-24)

Consider what your life would be like if it was described by what Paul calls "fruit of the Spirit." When we make contact with the Spirit of God, which in Michelangelo's painting is represented by air blowing the billowing drape that covers the Lord, we find that our lives are changed. When we exhibit these qualities, most messes simply don't occur in our lives. The ones that do occur get smaller. Some shrink away entirely. But it requires us to do something dramatic. Paul says we need to have "crucified the self with its passions and its desires," a level of commitment that sounds more like losing than gaining.

Idolatry

Our unwillingness to die to self—this tendency to lean away from God—is something the Bible calls idolatry. On a tour of Israel, I was able to visit Tel Dan, the place where King Jeroboam practiced idolatry by forging a golden calf. He offered it to the Israelites and told them it was the god that brought them up out of Egypt. Besides, he said, sacrificing to an idol at Tel Dan was easier than walking all the way to the temple in Jerusalem to worship the Lord.*

Such stories sound extreme to our ears. Idolatry, however, is alive and well today. I know that sounds harsh. We don't want to think of ourselves as idolaters. But idolatry occurs whenever a person gives excessive devotion or reveres someone or something in ways that give it ultimate meaning in his or her life. Many things can become idols: work, success, a relationship, a hobby or sport,

---

* In truth, Jeroboam gave the people an idol to keep his kingdom intact. He didn't want them to become faithful to King Rehoboam in Judah while they were at the temple in Jerusalem (1 Kings 12:26-29). In the excavated site at Tel Dan a sign denotes the area where the altar stood. Here sacrifices were made to a golden calf. The Bible records that people sometimes offered their firstborn children on such altars.

wealth, possessions, pride, ego. These can all become altars where we lay down our time, resources, and identity. This is when we lean away from God. Idolatry has to do with self-will and the desire to be our own boss rather than submit to the will of God. We worship what we think will bring us joy and meaning. We worship what we hope will bless us. Martin Luther is said to have observed, "Whatever your heart clings to and confides in, that is really your God."[1]

The problem with idols is that they disappoint us and lead to the creation of messes. The golden calf really does not bring a better harvest, no matter what you sacrifice to it. The bigger house you were hoping would improve your marriage ends up being just a bigger area to clean and a larger mortgage to pay. The whirlwind romance that pushes out friends and family turns into another dysfunctional relationship. The fixation on golf becomes the reason you never spend time with your two-year-old. A quick dalliance on the Internet turns out to be an addiction to porn. Idols can move rapidly from promise to mess.

Most of us don't engage in full-blown idolatry. People who are Christians do not typically reject God and go to pagan altars. Most of us have the kind of idolatry that's reflected on the face of Adam in Michelangelo's painting. It's the look of nonchalance, of seeing a relationship with God as one of many options. On a given Sunday morning there are many ways we can spend our time beyond a worship service. Likewise, decisions made at work or the way we treat a spouse or child may be centered more on how we feel on a given day than on what the Lord expects of us. Our words and actions, ethical decisions, and moral values arise from selfish desires rather than from the fruit of God's Spirit.

I call this lifestyle "high-functioning idolatry." I got this idea from recovery movements such as Alcoholics Anonymous, which often talk about high-functioning alcoholics.

Sarah Allen Benton is a licensed mental-health counselor and an alcoholic who has been in recovery for several years. She has written a book titled *Understanding the High-Functioning Alcoholic* (Praeger, 2009). As she describes them, high-functioning alcoholics are able to maintain respectable lives that look good to outsiders. Benton says that most high-functioning alcoholics are in denial about their abuse of alcohol. So are their social circles. The people around them, who also do not want to confront the often disappointing or abusive behavior, help to enable them. In a *New York Times* interview about her book, Benton says:

> High-functioning alcoholics are highly skilled at leading double lives. They appear to the outside world to be managing life well and defy the alcoholic stereotype by being fashionable, physically attractive, even elegant. They also tend to hide their excessive consumption by drinking alone or sneaking alcohol before or after a social event, and disguising or excusing the odor of alcohol on their breath.[2]

Similarly, high-functioning idolatry is when we look and sound a lot like devoted followers of Christ but have messes in our lives that indicate our commitment is not as deep as we thought. We may attend church and know a lot about the Bible, but when we look honestly at our lives, it's often clear that we are more self-driven than God-honoring.

Those of us who participate in high-functioning idolatry also live dual lives. We look good on the outside, give time to service, and may even participate in Bible study and worship, but we have an inner life that is very conflicted, along with habits and attitudes we know must be kept secret from others.

The result is a mess. As with the high-functioning alcoholic, everything is fine until it isn't. One day our lifestyle produces the crisis that forces us to examine who we are and where our allegiances really lie. The two different ways of living—our way and God's way—can't co-exist for very long.

> The two different ways of living—
> our way and God's way—
> can't co-exist for very long.

Perhaps we live this way because we know that if our Creator is ever allowed to fully grasp our hand, we will be changed forever. We will surrender control, and that will put an end to idols that we may be reluctant to release.

Author Henri Nouwen writes about the dilemma of setting aside idols in order to embrace God fully.

> The more I think about this the less surprised I am at our human resistance to let God be the Lord of our lives. Because God is a jealous lover (see 2 Corinthians 11:2) who wants to love every part of us with a divine love and wants to touch every one of our thoughts, words and actions, God is not content with a divided love in which we reserve parts of ourselves for ourselves or others. God does not want to be excluded from any corner of our heart. God wants the divine love to pervade every fibre of our being.

But we hesitate because such a lover might radically change us and lead us where we "would rather not go" (John 21:18).[3]

We are fortunate that God is patient with us. God loves us and continues to reach for us. God wants our full attention and shows us the way to a good life that's possible when God's image is restored within us.

Prevenient Grace

God works on us constantly, often in ways we don't recognize until later. John Wesley, founder of the Methodist movement, called this *prevenient grace.* Wesley believed that God tries to reach us long before we try to reach back. God's initiative is based solely on the desire to restore the image of God that lies under layers of sin and self-will within us. In his sermon titled "Working Out Our Own Salvation," Wesley wrote,

> Salvation begins with what is usually termed (and very properly) preventing grace; including the first wish to please God, the first dawn of light concerning his will, and the first slight transient conviction of having sinned against him. All these imply some tendency toward life; some degree of salvation; the beginning of a deliverance from a blind, unfeeling heart, quite insensible of God and the things of God.[4]

You can see prevenient grace at work in the account of Jesus' visit to Jericho and his meal with Zacchaeus in the Gospel of Luke.

Zacchaeus's life was a mess, but he probably wouldn't have described it that way if you had asked him about it. He had all the plates spinning. He was at the top of his profession—wealthy, successful, had a nice home and plenty of security. He was a good example of a high-functioning idolater. He was a Jew. Jesus called him *a son of Abraham*. He should have been serving God.

But Zacchaeus was a bad little man. He was a tax collector. This was not a parable Jesus made up. It was his real life. Zacchaeus collected taxes for Rome. In fact, he was the head tax collector in Jericho, a good-sized city in those days but small enough that he would have been known by everyone. He was rich on money wrung from his neighbors' hard work. He was hated by most and welcomed by few.

We have to ask how Zacchaeus became a tax collector. Does anyone set out to have a profession for which they are hated, isolated, and despised? When he was a child, did Zacchaeus think, *One day when I grow up, I want to extort innocent people out of their hard-earned money on behalf of the occupying empire*?

Perhaps Zacchaeus's willingness to get rich at any cost was passed down from his parents. Sometimes our mess, and the inclination to set the wrong priorities, is modeled to us by those who raise us. Many counselors ask new clients to trace their family tree and describe the people and relationships in it as a way of identifying the context for the issues and problems in their lives. A family tree that uses colors and symbols to map emotional connections and relational patterns of a family system is called a genogram. In some instances it could be called a family mess map. If you fill out a genogram, you can begin to see that much of the mess you are trying to fix is similar to the mess your parents, grandparents, and other members of your family have dealt with in the past. It turns out that we pass down a whole lot more than quilts and Grandma's china.

It is also possible that Zacchaeus created his own mess despite the best efforts of a loving family who modeled solid ethical and moral values. That happens to us as well. Sometimes when your life is a mess, there is simply no one to blame but yourself. You can talk poorly of your parents and disparage your siblings, spouse, friends, florist, barber, meteorologist, tattoo artist, or anyone else you can think of, but when you are honest, this one was all you.

We don't know Zacchaeus's past. We do know that God had a desire to change his future and help him discover his true identity, because Zacchaeus's story includes all the signs of God's prevenient grace.

Initiative

The account begins this way: "Jesus entered Jericho and was passing through town" (Luke 19:1). It sounds as if Jesus was just out for a stroll, like he had nowhere else to go but Jericho. It is true that Jesus toured town after town and looked for people to teach and help. Everywhere he went, there was someone who had a mess. (Not much has changed in two thousand years, has it?) But in the account we learn that Jesus knew about Zacchaeus.

> *A man there named Zacchaeus, a ruler among tax collectors, was rich. He was trying to see who Jesus was, but, being a short man, he couldn't because of the crowd. So he ran ahead and climbed up a sycamore tree so he could see Jesus, who was about to pass that way. When Jesus came to that spot, he looked up and said, "Zacchaeus, come down at once. I must stay in your home today."*
>
> (Luke 19:2-5)

Zacchaeus did not know Jesus, but Jesus surely knew him.

Timing

I think something must have been going on in Zacchaeus's life. He was searching for something or he would not have gone to the effort to climb a tree. Think of how ridiculous he looked. This rich, prominent man, a person feared by others, ran down the street in his best tunic and climbed a tree.

Jesus always seemed to show up at just the right time for people. It happened over and over again in Scripture: when a man's daughter had just died; when a boy was falling on the ground in convulsions; when a woman was about to be stoned to death for adultery; when a Roman army captain's servant became ill; when a woman was desperate because she had been sick and bleeding for years and years; when the disciples were in a boat, and a storm came out of nowhere.

God wants to convince you that
you are valued and loved and can
be forgiven and changed,
no matter what.

Jesus has timing, and that timing has a name: prevenient grace. God is always searching for you, trying to get your attention, reminding you that no matter what your story is or what a mess you have made, God is there, ready to help you begin a new chapter. God wants to convince you that you are valued and loved and can be forgiven and changed, no matter what.

Even when you have given up, God has not. In fact, it is often when we give up that Jesus starts up. Jesus doesn't care that others have given up on you or are afraid they will be hurt by you. Jesus just barges right in, inviting himself into your life, offering you things you can't buy and giving you things you don't deserve. Jesus doesn't care what other people think. And he knows you, even if you don't know him.

I wonder how Jesus knew Zacchaeus. Maybe Jesus knew him by his terrible reputation. Or maybe, since Jesus is the Messiah, he knows everything about Zacchaeus and you and me. So often we think God is out in the cosmos somewhere, distant and aloof. What if right now the Lord is actually calling your name but you are so focused on other things you can't hear it?

Often we think that God is not active because we are too distracted to see God at work. We are so stuck in our rut that we can't see anything but the spinning tires. We complain, "How can God leave me here? Can't God see that I need help? Why am I so alone?" But this speaks more to the limit of our vision than to the nature of God's love.

God is a seeking God. Christ is called Savior because he comes to us when we least expect him and most need him. This is why many people, when describing their faith journey, will say that a conversation with someone happened at just the right time. Or they were driving past a church on a Sunday, felt moved to go inside, and heard just the sermon they needed to hear.

People routinely experience the good timing of God's grace. When Zacchaeus climbed the tree, he was ready for something to happen in his life, and it did: "So Zacchaeus came down at once, happy to welcome Jesus" (Luke 19:6).

Relationship

In almost every culture, it is out of the social norm to invite yourself to a stranger's home. But Jesus did it as though Zacchaeus had been waiting for the opportunity to host him. Jesus made what many call a *divine appointment* with Zacchaeus.

Jesus wanted to visit Zacchaeus's home so the two of them could have a conversation and a relationship. He wanted to share a meal, knowing that in that culture, sharing a meal with someone meant becoming a part of their family, if only for a short time. Jesus knew that the more of a relationship Zacchaeus experienced, the more likely he was to experience restoration.

Jesus also knew that restoration takes time. This can be a hard concept for people born in the West to understand. We tend to think of salvation as a single transaction. God is the judge, and we are the defendants who have made a mess in our lives. If your goal is to get into heaven, this is a helpful understanding of grace. It has limits, however, if your desire is to experience salvation as something that changes you and brings new life this side of heaven.

Theologian Randy Maddox points out that John Wesley's view of grace is helpful. Wesley takes the Western view of salvation as a single transaction and yokes it with an Eastern view that grace restores and renews us over time. Using both concepts, Wesley describes God's grace as forgiveness granted at one essential moment, followed by a healing process that occurs over time.[5]

We might compare the forgiveness to surgery and the healing process to physical therapy. The initial surgery is essential, but without the follow-up therapy, scar tissue can form that can limit mobility and bring back the pain experienced before surgery.

Prevenient grace begins with a relationship because the process requires it. You may only meet your surgeon once or twice before surgery takes place, whereas you will see your physical therapist so often that you may come to know the person by name. If the need is great enough, you will visit them for weeks. That same kind of ongoing relationship with God will be necessary in order for grace to result in our full restoration.

Awakening

Perhaps the most important function of prevenient grace is to awaken us to the distant memory of God's love for us, and the value we hold as one created in God's image. Ted Runyon is helpful here: "In Christ Jesus God chooses all humanity for renewal in that destiny for which all were created, to be the very image of God. And prevenient grace seeks to awaken every human being to that possibility."[6]

We don't know what Jesus said to Zacchaeus or what they discussed over dinner that day. Meals in the first century took a long time. They had to be cooked slowly over a fire, so no one ate quickly. There would have been a lot of time for Jesus and Zacchaeus to talk. Maybe Zacchaeus wondered aloud how he had become the man he was. Jesus could have given him confidence about the man he could be. Or maybe Zacchaeus simply began to believe in God again. Here I don't mean belief as a simple intellectual assent to a set of dogmas; I mean awakening or reawakening to faith. Jesus may have convinced him that God was real, cared for him, and could enable Zacchaeus to enter a new life.

I think sometimes our messes cover us so deeply that we forget our Creator. Then something stirs our memory and awakens us, like hearing a tune and recalling a song from years past, or smelling a fragrance and following it to the neighbor's grill. We can imagine Jesus leading Zacchaeus to a flash of insight and recognition that changed everything.

Participation

We can see Jesus' power in Zacchaeus's response: Zacchaeus gave half his wealth to the poor and promised to return four times the amount he took from people. He had found a way to participate in changing his story. Make no mistake, Jesus could have forced Zacchaeus to change. If Jesus could walk on water, raise the dead, and heal the sick, he could have made a self-serving tax collector cough up the cash to repay his victims. Jesus could even have done that move Obi-Wan Kenobi did to the Stormtroopers—a wave of the fingers, a *These aren't the droids you are looking for,* and all would have been well.

God doesn't overpower us with grace, but simply offers it.

But that's not how God works. God doesn't overpower us with grace, but simply offers it. God does not start our restoration until we have signed off on the project. It's a partnership and a shared journey, not a forced march. Just as a surgeon can't force us to do our physical therapy, so God is unwilling to restore God's image within us until we provide our consent and active participation. St. Augustine probably captured this best when he wrote, "He who made us without ourselves, will not save us without ourselves."[7]

In speaking of Zacchaeus, Jesus made a pronouncement that helps us see his understanding of salvation: "Today, salvation has come to this household because he too is a son of Abraham" (Luke 19:9).

For Jesus, salvation is not about getting our ticket punched so we can get into heaven. Salvation is about an earthly life that leads to eternal life. It affects how we treat each other now, and how we embody and express God's image to our loved ones and community.

At some point, Adam will have to lean toward the Almighty to bridge the gap between them. So will you and I.

Community

One final note about prevenient grace: it's not all about you. Though it's essential to understand that God knows and loves each one of us, that "even the hairs on your head are all counted" (a job that in my case is getting easier for the Lord every year), we often get too focused on ourselves when we consider God's desire for our transformation. Yes, God wants you to experience new life, but God also wants new life for everyone with whom you are connected.

In this era of social media, the idea of connection is easy to understand. On Facebook you can discover that a high school friend you haven't seen in years is in the same social network as your co-worker, who knew her in college. It turns out the two of them are connected to another friend you met on vacation a few years ago. It's crazy how connected we all are. God knows about these connections. When God is working to change your life, the big goal is to change the life of everyone in your network.

God wants to share grace broadly and socially, not just inwardly and individually. There were a lot of people Jesus could have spent time with in Jericho, because undoubtedly there was a lot of mess in that city. Maybe Jesus spent a disproportionate time with Zacchaeus that day because he knew that if the chief tax collector gave his life to God and turned away from corruption, everybody's life would get better.

Jesus' purpose is not just to fill heaven one person at a time; it is also to change the life that will change the town that will change the community, so the world will become better here and now.

Grace and Transformation

After decades of full-time pastoral ministry, here is what I know: People will not deal with their sin until they believe in the unconditional love of God and those around them. That's why a theology of grace is essential to transformation. You must believe that you are loved no matter what, that love is God's gift and pursuit, before you will look at yourself completely and openly, trusting that God will only use you for good.

What if the Holy Spirit is doing this prevenient grace thing in your life right now? What if God is trying to get your attention and remind you that love and grace are available to you? Many see the work of restoration as a hard season of examination, divine recrimination, and personal guilt. But what if it is something totally different?

Last winter we had a lot of snow. It came over a number of weeks from different storms. The snow was so consistent that our snow blower finally snorted to a stop and refused to be resuscitated. The last snow came down pretty fast. Driving home from work

I saw people slip and slide around in their cars, including one person who had an accident. When I got home, I had to do a lot of shoveling to get my car up the hill and into the garage. It was a mess. The restoration process is like that. It is a cold season in which we have to shovel and scrape. Sometimes we get stuck and have to get towed out of a ditch.

But the next morning when I awoke, the first thing I heard was a bird. A robin was singing. At first I thought it might be complaining about the cold and ice. As I lay there and listened, I realized that the robin was not complaining at all. It was calling out a reminder that spring was on the way. It was telling us that God was about to disrupt the story of our long winter to bring light and sun and warmth and new life.

This is the nature of God's love and grace—always searching, seeking, and showing up at the right time to lead us from a mess to a place of light and hope. It's the work of prevenient grace, and it's what will lead us to the next phase of the journey.

3

BLESS THIS MESS

For all have sinned and fall short of the glory of God, and all are justified freely by his grace through the redemption that came by Christ Jesus.

(Romans 3:23-24 NIV)

Recently I read about a man who was on his way to Syria. I think it's fair to call him an extremist. The man had strong convictions about his faith and no tolerance for infidels. He strictly adhered to his religion. He worked to put citizens in jail who do not practice the religion common to his country. On at least one occasion he incited a mob to kill a man because of the man's religious beliefs. No arrest, no hearing—they just stoned the man to death in an open field. Like religious extremists everywhere, he was not open to conversation, correction, or debate about what he saw as the truth. He was hard. From our point of view, he was a total mess.

You can read all about this guy. You'll find his story in the Book of Acts. His name was Saul of Tarsus. On his way to Damascus, Jesus appeared to Saul in a vision and asked why Saul was persecuting him. A lot happened after that, but here is the short version: Jesus changed Saul's life. Today we know him as the Apostle Paul. Paul ended up writing the majority of the New Testament. If God could change that guy and move his passion in a new direction, God can change any of us.

But How?

When we deal with the question of transformation in our lives, we have to deal with at least two issues: (1) What has the power to change us? (2) Do we want to change?

We are not just talking about any change here. This is about the restoration of our identity and life. Author Richard Foster reminds us that there are two Greek words used in Scripture for life: *bios*, which means physical or mortal life; and *zoe*, which refers to spiritual or eternal life. There are also two Greek words for death: *teleute*, or physical death; and *thanatos*, or spiritual death. Foster writes,

> Thus, it is entirely possible for a person to be physically alive (*bios*) while spiritually dead (*thanatos*). But the salvation that is in Jesus Christ immerses us into the hidden reservoir of divine love and power, bringing into our lives God's life (*zoe*) and forming us into communities of Jesus' disciples.[1]

The goal of the Christian life is not just making a few changes along the way. Entering into life in Christ is not about giving up a bad habit, such as biting your nails or being grumpy when you sleep poorly. It is not about overcoming a character defect, such as telling occasional lies or losing control of your temper. It is about the journey of a lifetime. We must understand, writes Foster, "that God is not seeking to improve us, but to transform us—to show us who he really created us to be."[2]

It sounds like wonderfully good news that such change might be possible, but there is a hard truth to consider. Many of us don't want to change. There is comfort in familiarity. Even though we know that that comfort is less than the good God desires for us, it is a way of being that we know well and may not want to leave behind. Sometimes our train has come to a halt at dysfunction junction, and we don't feel like getting up enough steam to get out of there. We may long for a better life and even lament the hardships and struggles that our sins bring, but we don't necessarily want God to give us something truly new and truly different.

We may long for a better life…but we don't necessarily want God to give us something truly new and truly different.

I once saw a sign that hung over a man's desk that read, *Bless this mess.* I asked the man why it was there, and he said, "I used to pray that I would be more organized until I saw that sign. Now I pray that God will just bless my mess." I don't know if God was blessing his mess, but as I took in the piles of junk on his desk, floor, filing cabinets, end tables, and chairs, I saw that he was giving the Lord plenty of opportunity.

Bless this mess. I have seen that sign in many places over the years, in kitchens, basements, garages, and other disordered spaces. Sometimes we hang the sign over the messy parts of our lives as well. Sin creates a lot of chaos and confusion in our lives. Rather than seeking transformation and surrendering our way to God's design for life, we ask God to "bless this mess." Using the phrase could mean that we want God to ignore the mess. It could also mean that we want God magically to fix it.

When Derek and Nina get home from an evening out, they often discuss the size of their friends' home, what art decorated the walls, and what type of cars they drive. They talk about what they would need to do in order to own these things. They complain about the unfairness of life. They usually end up feeling bad about their possessions and less content with each other. One night, on the drive home from dinner with some friends, Nina notices this pattern and suggests that they switch the topic of conversation. She recognizes the sin of envy in their lives. The pastor talked about it on Sunday, and she realizes it's not a healthy way to live.

The next few moments are spent in silence. They each try to start a conversation, but it goes nowhere. More silence. Then Derek says something about what a good meal it was, what a great job grilling Jay did, and what a nice grill he was using. "Did you notice the temperature control?" asks Derek. "It was perfect. And there was a rotisserie feature." Before long, they are discussing the slate patio and the comfortable chair cushions. Derek says, "I know I should stop talking about it, but did you notice how nice that table was?" With that, they are off on a virtual tour of the house.

This is an example of "Bless this mess" thinking. We want to change, but unless God waves a magic wand, change isn't going to happen. It's not enough to identify the problem and try to do better. Real change requires power that we don't have on our own. It's an act of surrender and a series of prayerful requests for God's help. If we try to change on our own, we may decide that the mess we identified wasn't actually a mess. We know that others call it a sin, but suddenly it doesn't seem so bad. Besides, we're used to it, and its familiar pattern defines us. It's the way we do life.

"Bless this mess" thinking isn't limited to our personal lives; it's a way of seeing the world. I once talked with a teenager who had been on a mission trip in South America. She had distributed food in a very poor region that could not have been more different from the safe, comfortable suburb where she was raised. She was appalled by the lack of clean drinking water, the disrepair of the homes, and the children's lack of access to education. She asked angrily, "Why would God do this to them?"

She and I had a long conversation about structural evil, government corruption, colonial legacy, and the economics of poverty and privilege. I wanted her to understand that what she observed was not God's doing, but the sins of humanity played out generation after generation. It was not God who had done poorly by those children. Their neighborhood had been carefully crafted, decade by decade, century by century, by countless sins of commission and omission. Too often, we hang a "Bless this mess" sign over the entrance gate of such communities, in the hope that God will get busy with a miracle while we walk away.

In our personal lives and in the world, if we ignore a mess too long it will take over. That's the nature of sin. We must understand this about sin or we will never take it seriously, and our lives will continue to be plagued by the symptoms of our illness.

The Stink Bug

Walking up the stairs in our home, I had just reached the top step when something caught my eye. It was a stink bug, the first of the season.

I really dislike stink bugs. Some call them shield bugs, but I think that grants them too much dignity. Stink bugs come into the quiet spaces of our homes in the late fall, looking for shelter and warmth. They hang out there for some time. However, I'm happy to say that the stink bug on our bannister didn't last long.

I was disheartened to see the stink bug but realized it could have been worse. I read about Doug Inkley, who was overrun by stink bugs. Doug swears that he once had over eight thousand in his house. He vacuumed them up and counted them. Then he got busy. Doug filled gaps in his siding and used over thirty tubes of caulk. He invested ten thousand dollars in new windows. After all that effort, the stink bugs were still everywhere. When Doug sees a stink bug, he knows it is *not* to be ignored!

This is because stink bugs never travel alone. They are *legion*. The odor they emit is bad, and they can do real harm. Orchard growers and farmers know the damage they bring to crops. Stink bugs get on fruit and vegetables and puncture the surface to get what they want. Their puncture wounds create bruises and dimples that lower the fruit's value, rob it of its natural beauty, and invite disease.[3]

I interviewed people about stink bugs to get my facts straight. Okay, it was only four people, but I think they nailed it. Here is what they said about stink bugs:

- They are always there.
- They keep coming back.

- They go places they do not belong.
- They come out of nowhere and land right on you.
- The stink sticks with you. If you touch them, you wear stink-bug cologne all day.
- I can't beat them no matter how hard I try.

When I heard those responses, it occurred to me that the sins we commit are the stink bugs of our souls. When you touch a stink bug the odor will get all over you, and the effect of sin is much the same. Sins puncture our character, bruise our integrity, damage our beauty, compromise our relationships, and harm our well-being. Consider for a moment the way sins affect your life, relationships, work, time, and ability to function well each day. How do sins affect your physical health? your emotional state? your sense of spiritual vitality?

Sins puncture our character, bruise our integrity, damage our beauty, compromise our relationships, and harm our well-being.

A married couple had a quarrel and gave each other the silent treatment. Both refused to talk, extend forgiveness, or offer a compromise. A week into their noiseless argument, the man realized he needed his wife's help. He was not an early riser, but he had to get up at 4 a.m. to catch a flight for a business meeting.

Not wanting to be the first to break the silence, the man wrote on a piece of paper, "Please make sure I'm up at 4 a.m."

The next morning, the man woke up only to discover that his wife was already out of bed. It was 8 a.m., and his flight had long since departed. He was about to find his wife and demand an answer for her failings when he noticed a piece of paper by the bed.

He read, "It's 4 a.m. Wake up."

That couple has a load of stink bugs.

Justifying Grace

None of us can escape sin. Here's how Paul put it in Romans 3:23: "All have sinned and fall short of God's glory...."

All is an inclusive, fully comprehensive term. Reading it in Paul's letter, there's no way to see ourselves as exempt from the condition or different from others. And, sad to say, the range of sin doesn't seem to have diminished since Paul's time. In fact, sin seems to be doing just fine. You might say it's a growth sector of the world's moral economy.

In their book *Freakonomics*, economists Steven D. Levitt and Stephen J. Dubner provide a vivid example of this trend in their discussion of just one sin: cheating. Levitt and Dubner write that cheating is "a prominent feature in just about every human endeavor."[4] They note that cheating can be found everywhere in our society, including in job categories that typically are associated with keeping rules, such as schoolteacher. Teachers are most tempted to cheat when their pupils test scores are low.

Does that sound strangely familiar? It should. Levitt and Dubner point out what happened in 1987. On a spring night, when the clock moved one second past midnight, seven million American children disappeared. It was not a massive alien abduction. It was April 16, the first day of the tax year, when a new

Internal Revenue Service rule went into effect. Starting that day, parents were required to enter the Social Security number beside the name of any child they claimed as a dependent for the purpose of a tax exemption. That change to the income tax form had a startling result. Suddenly, seven million children across the United States simply vanished. One-tenth of all dependent children in the country were gone! The military was not alerted. Police were not called out for duty. No sirens wailed. Taxpayers just took a step toward greater honesty.[5]

If *all* is all in Scripture, with social science providing affirmation, we have to ask if anything has the power to rid humans of their predilection to break the rules and serve themselves. The answer is *yes*! This is what God does through the power of justifying grace.

Grace is a word that we assume to be positive. It is defined as the free gift of God's unmerited love for us. When I receive a gift, I usually feel great about it. Sometimes the gift comes because I did something to earn it, such as a free night's stay at a hotel after accruing sufficient points in a rewards program. Other gifts come because of an occasion, such as a birthday or Christmas. God's grace is a different sort of gift. It is unmerited favor shown to us by a benevolent Creator who is always willing to see us as the persons we can become. That divine view allows us to experience transformation and then not only receive grace ourselves but extend it to others.

We learned that prevenient grace—God's grace in our lives before we are even aware of it—opens our eyes to God's love and desire to close the gap that sin has created in our lives. God's next step, *justifying grace*, seeks to show us who we are. When John Newton wrote the words to "Amazing Grace," he was thanking God for the gift of justifying grace.

> Amazing grace! How sweet the sound that saved
>   a wretch like me!
> I once was lost, but now am found; was blind but
>   now I see.

Newton thought grace was amazing because it showed him that he was a wretch, spiritually lost, and morally blind.

That does not sound like a gift anyone would be anxious to open. Essentially, Newton unwrapped the gift of God's grace, and when he looked inside the box he saw a true portrait of himself rather than the false image he had created. Newton was a slave trader. He was guilty of terrible crimes against humanity including abduction, rape, torture, and human trafficking, just to name a few. During the time he was involved in the slave trade, if you had asked him what he did for a living he might have said he was a ship's captain and businessman involved in import and export. One day, however, God opened his eyes to the truth about himself. He realized that he was destroying lives and families, and he grasped the horror and inhumanity of his actions. The new vision that God gave to John Newton was a gift.

Grace, he realized, was amazing.

If you are like me, right now you are thinking, *Well, at least I'm not like that guy.* That isn't grace talking; it's the voice of the functional idolater who does not understand God's gift of justifying grace. It's the fear that if Newton's experience of God's justifying grace comes our way, it will expose some things in our lives that you and I don't want to see.

An accurate diagnosis is essential to the process. That's why lives cannot be transformed without the presence of justifying grace. Even though I may not be John Newton, I must remember that *all* have sinned and fallen short of God's glory. Remembering and accepting that truth allows me to embrace God's justifying grace as the means to see my mess, name it, and allow the transformation to begin. This is true for you, me, and everybody else.

One critical aspect of justifying grace is the gift of awareness. It enables us to see that we are out of alignment with God's ways, and it's essential if we are to gain the life that Christ desires for us. If we are to be found, as Newton wrote, we must first see that we are lost. That takes us back to the question of whether we really *want* to be found. If we are to receive grace and be transformed through its power, we have to be a part of the process.

Repentance and Confession

We are fortunate that God is both merciful and patient. Justifying grace first opens our eyes to our condition; then, when we begin to long for change, that same grace is present to help us heal over time.[6]

Repentance is the outcome of justifying grace. After we realize that we've gone in the wrong direction, repentance is the experience of turning around. It occurs when we recognize that, with our help, God will heal and restore us to the image of God in which we were created. If we long for the new life that God offers us, we can be forgiven of our past.

Repentance is both a one-time event and a process of transformation over time. It is the moment when our eyes are opened to our sin, as well as the ongoing process of change in our lives, demonstrated in the goals and desires we pursue. It means being willing to make a thorough examination of our lives. Repentance occurs when we realize that our old life is not a good life and begin working, with grace, to find something new.

When I was a teenager, a friend in our neighborhood restored a 1957 Chevrolet. As a young man, our friend had worked and saved enough money to order the model he wanted from the factory. When the truck pulled into the car dealership carrying his two-door, turquoise-and-ivory Bel Air, it was love at first sight. The truck driver allowed him to drive the car off the carrier so he could say he was the only person ever to have driven it. And indeed, he drove that car for years. After many miles, he stored it in a barn.

The car sat there for twelve to fifteen years, and then our friend towed it into a garage and began to work on it. His goal was to get it in top condition so he could compete in car shows. He didn't just hit the highlights. He didn't polish a bumper and call it a day. The restoration project was long and methodical, even painstakingly tedious. The outside of the car was disassembled, part by part. Fenders were removed, sanded, repainted, and reinstalled. The interior was cleaned and repaired. Under the hood, hoses were replaced. Parts were cleaned and thoroughly inspected. Everything, down to the nuts and bolts, was removed, cleaned, repaired, painted, or replaced. It was a thorough and complete process. Our friend took this much time and effort because his goal was not just to improve the car or make it driveable; he wanted to restore the vehicle in such a way that people would experience the same "wow" he had felt that first day at the dealership.

The transformation of our lives requires a similar attention to detail. We must desire more than a quick stroke of grace that will get us up and moving. The renewal of God's image requires us to get down to the nuts and bolts of our actions, attitudes, and habits. God is patient and thorough in the process.

Part of this process involves confession. The practice of confession is one of the great disciplines of the Christian life. For justifying grace to bring real healing, we must confess our sins and repent of them. With God's help we identify the places where we are out of alignment with God and then ask God to change us in these areas. If you have ever experienced or read about a twelve-step program, you will recognize the fourth and fifth steps that participants go through:

> 4. Made a searching and fearless moral inventory of ourselves.
> 5. Admitted to God, to ourselves, and to another human being the exact nature of our wrongs.[7]

Many of us fear confession, even if it simply means praying privately to God. We prefer to pretend that all is well and to focus on matters that don't embarrass us or that we can easily change on our own. The power of confession is that it requires us to examine all aspects of our lives. To accomplish Step 5, you have to go though Step 4. When we make a searching and fearless moral inventory of ourselves, we begin to work with God in a highly synergistic way.

The power of confession is that it requires us to examine all aspects of our lives.

This is where justifying grace continues its work. The Holy Spirit enables us to see what we did not want to admit previously. Note that the inventory must be fearless if it is to be comprehensive.

We must be more concerned about changing than about preserving our self-image. To confess our sins is the ultimate act of trust in God. It is the highest expression of belief in God's love for us. It says that we can be vulnerable before God, trusting in God's mercy and forbearance. Many do not want to be this vulnerable, even when alone with God in prayer. We fear that God will condemn us or give us the punishment that we believe we deserve.

Confessing means having faith that God is, above all, compassionate toward us. God knows our weaknesses. God is not to be feared, because Christ longs to restore us to the joy of God's presence. And by the way, when you confess a sin to the Almighty, you are not giving the Lord any fresh news. The realization that you're a hothead may be a lightning bolt to some people, but God knew about it some time ago, along with the rest of your sins.

I was curious about the use of confession in the Roman Catholic tradition. I realize that some Roman Catholics associate confession with deep feelings of guilt for past actions. But talking with a neighboring Roman Catholic priest, I learned that he used the term *Rite of Reconciliation* to describe the practice. The goal, he explained, is not simply to confess and certainly not to feel bad. The goal is to find reconciliation with God, others, and ultimately ourselves. Not only does it lead us to become honest with God; it calls us to change our ways and make amends with those we have hurt or wounded. Confession is not about enduring the heat of God's wrath, but about being cleansed of guilt so we can live a new life.

The Man at the Pool

Jesus met a man in Jerusalem who was unable to walk, or perhaps did so with great difficulty. Think of how hard life in first-century Palestine would be if you had trouble walking. Jerusalem was a city built on a hillside. There were crowds, lots of stone steps without handrails, and no adaptive devices or access ramps to assist mobility. People might have had crutches, but there were no walkers or wheelchairs yet. Jesus came across this man at the pool of Bethsaida. People with disabilities went to the pool to be healed, and given the lack of an alternative, we can imagine they would make it a priority to be there. They believed that from time to time an angel would come to the pool, stir up the water, and the first person in the water after the angel departed would be healed.

Here is what we know about the man Jesus encountered: "One who was there had been an invalid for thirty-eight years" (John 5:5 NIV). This is a guy who had learned to tolerate his condition. For thirty-eight years he had lain there on sunny days, rainy days, hot days, and cold days, perhaps lacking either the creativity or the will to figure out how to make his life any different.

The man's outlook is not uncommon. It's often easier to endure a bad situation and hope for a magic blessing than pray for the clarity of God's justifying grace to reveal the truth about ourselves. This tendency expresses itself in many ways. Bad marriages continue for decades without any attempt to talk with a pastor or counselor, to read a book on marriage, or to attend a seminar on healthy relationships. Compulsions such as shoplifting or the use of porn can go on for years. Sins such as swearing or fornication, which many Christians in the United States are comfortable with in their private time, are overlooked. We settle for less than God's best for our lives, continuing to accept our sin even as we endure the guilt, conflict, and hardships they produce. If we would dive deeply into the life Christ offers us, his power would change us.

Instead we lie by the pool, hoping that change will come on its own and that one day God might choose to bless our mess.

Sometimes our inattention to these issues can lead to a level of conflict and personal loss that is commonly called *hitting bottom*. This is when life becomes so unmanageable that we can no longer ignore the mess and are forced to make some change. The change may not be self-initiated; hitting bottom often happens when people around us become so weary of our dysfunctional patterns that they remove their support from us. It can be painful. We feel unloved. Self-pity tells us that no one cares for us. In truth, when others walk away we often don't miss them as much as the ways they inadvertently enabled our dysfunctional lifestyle. Hitting bottom is gut-wrenching, but sometimes it's needed for God's justifying grace to enter our lives.

Hitting bottom is gut-wrenching, but sometimes it's needed for God's justifying grace to enter our lives.

When Jesus saw the man lying at the pool, he had one simple question. It didn't require an essay response, not even multiple choice, just yes or no. In spite of the question's simplicity, however, the answer held the key to the man's future. It's the key to ours as well.

Jesus asked, "Do you want to get well?" (John 5:6).

The question was crucial, because it required the man to accept that he was sick. The first step on the path to healing and transformation is acknowledgment of a mess. The second is accurately diagnosing its source and doing what is required to become well. In Jesus' question was the implication that Jesus had the cure to the malady. But first the man had to admit that he was interested in receiving it. He had to be willing to do what Jesus asked of him. This is the partnership that the gift of grace offers. There is the hope and confidence that God can deliver us, and there is the covenant we enter into when we receive God's grace that we will respond as God directs.

In John's account, though, instead of answering, "Yes, I would like to be made well," the man offered excuses.

> *The sick man answered him, "Sir, I don't have anyone who can put me in the water when it is stirred up. When I'm trying to get to it, someone else has gotten in ahead of me."*
>
> (John 5:7)

The man was stuck in his illness. He wanted Jesus to know that he had a good reason for not seeking a cure, even if a miraculous one might be just a few cubits away: he had no one to help him. It's tempting to believe that the man was a victim of an uncaring family, or that prejudice about disabilities in his society made it hard for him to build friendships. We can't really know, but we do know Jesus' response.

> *Jesus said to him, "Get up! Pick up your mat and walk." Immediately the man was well, and he picked up his mat and walked. Now that day was the Sabbath.*
>
> (John 5:8-9)

Jesus' words proved that grace is indeed a gift. And the fact that the miracle occurred on the Sabbath is significant. The main thing we see is that the man was able to walk for the first time in thirty-eight years; but the religious leaders in Jerusalem, where the temple was located, only saw that the man had violated the Sabbath by carrying his mat on the holy day. Both the mat-carrier and the person who did the miracle were in violation of Sabbath laws and merited reprimands. In spite of this, Jesus went out on a limb for the man, highlighting God's willingness to offer us grace that transforms our lives.

Notice that the man did not thank Jesus. He didn't ask if he could follow Jesus. He didn't tell anyone else about Jesus, even those who were right around him. His lack of concern for others who shared his condition is most notable. One might have thought he would have made a few friends in his thirty-eight–year stay by the pool of Bethsaida. We can imagine him falling at Jesus' feet, begging him to help others gathered there. But the Scripture says the man gathered up his mat and took off. Apparently he walked away from the healing pool, onto the streets of Jerusalem, and never looked back.

Jesus saw the man later and tried to open his eyes a bit: "See! You have been made well. Don't sin anymore in case something worse happens to you" (John 5:14).

The man's life had been changed. He was able to walk normally after decades of not being able to do so. What a shame that he didn't use the healing to experience a full transformation of his life. If he had asked, surely Jesus would have helped the man overcome the habits, attitudes, and thinking that had limited his life in so many other ways.

Jesus' final concern for the man was that he would not sin anymore. I wonder if the man recognized what Jesus meant: that while God has the power to change us by himself, he requires us to be participants in our healing. That means looking at our lives with the eyes of Christ. These are the eyes not of judgment but of discernment. We must be thorough and not overlook sin that contributes to our bad physical, mental, emotional, or spiritual health. We must recognize that God doesn't want to bless our mess; he wants to fix it, with our help.

4

NO MESSING AROUND

May God himself, the God of peace, sanctify you through and through. May your whole spirit, soul and body be kept blameless at the coming of our Lord Jesus Christ. The one who calls you is faithful, and he will do it.

(1 Thessalonians 5:23-24 NIV)

One Sunday not long ago, the people in our congregation opened their bulletins to find small, heart-shaped pieces of paper with adhesive backing. I asked people to write down a sin they wanted to tell God about. It could be an event they regretted, a habit they could not shake, or something bigger. People took some time to think and then began to write things on the sticky hearts. Then I invited them to come down front, toward the large cross in our sanctuary. Over the course of our four Sunday services, hundreds of people came forward, knelt, and laid their words of confession on the railing. Some prayed alone. Others waited for someone to pray with them.

People had been told that any notes left on the railing would be posted in the atrium outside the chapel so that others could read them and understand that we are all in the same struggle. After each service, we gathered up those notes and formed them into a couple of large heart patterns. These hearts held the changes that people want to make. These words listed the issues we struggle with because we have not allowed the grace of God to work in our lives. We suffer because these sins are present.

The notes included statements such as

- Losing my temper with my family
- Hurting others with my words
- Alcohol, food, and other addictions
- Lack of compassion
- Judging others
- Being unkind
- Gossip
- Holding grudges
- Unwillingness to forgive
- Envy
- Condemnation
- Lying
- Cheating

Reading the notes made me realize again that all of us share a common problem: our souls are warped. They are bent in ways we did not plan or intend.

Recently I went to the local home-improvement store to buy some two-by-fours for shelving in our garage. I picked up a few boards and realized that they were neither straight nor true. They warped left or right, up or down. One by one I looked down the length of the boards. If they were straight, I put them on my cart. If they were warped, I cast them aside. A man beside me was doing the same thing. He needed boards that were nearly perfect. Mine could have a slight variance, but neither of us wanted to pay for a truly warped board. We didn't want to go through the hassle of forcing a warped board to conform to the specifications called for in our plans.

God enables us to see ourselves as we really are, with all our warps and misalignments, and God delights in making us new.

Like those boards, we are warped. But here is the good news: God does not cast us aside. God gives us the gift of justifying grace. God enables us to see ourselves as we really are, with all our warps and misalignments, and God delights in making us new. The primary way God does this is through the gift of the Bible's wisdom and its account of Jesus' life and teaching and his death and resurrection, which are the standard of a life that fully reflects the presence of God in a sin-filled world.

Jesus enables us to see a new standard of existence. No warps. No misalignments. Jesus is straight and true, showing us the beauty of God's image unhindered by layers of sin. When we look at his life and examine our own, we long for change. Suddenly our practices of idolatry and self-glorification don't seem worthy of attention. Our idols are exposed for the worthless junk they are, and instead we desire to cooperate with God to be brought into alignment with God's love and God's ways. We long for a life that reflects the beauty and righteousness of Christ. Paul puts it this way: "Therefore, since we have been made righteous through his faithfulness, we have peace with God through our Lord Jesus Christ" (Romans 5:1).

Sin and the Mess It Creates

A key to this experience is to give up thinking that we can change on our own. We aren't going to become the person God wants us to be by working harder or attending the right seminar. To truly change, we have to realize that the board, created straight and true but warped over time, can't justify and align itself. We have to surrender the belief that we can change ourselves and instead turn fully to the power of Christ's transforming love. Paul writes, "This hope doesn't put us to shame, because the love of God has been poured out in our hearts through the Holy Spirit, who has been given to us" (Romans 5:5).

Through justifying grace, Christ works in our lives to help us see our habits, relationships, and life goals for what they are. The Holy Spirit is on the journey with us, enabling us to experience the forgiveness of our sins and the restoration of God's image within us.

When the Holy Spirit is present, we have a far deeper understanding of what motivates our lives and how we affect others. Our conscience, acting alone, might be able to tell that something is amiss, in the same way that someone experiencing pain knows something is wrong. The person might ignore the pain or try an over-the-counter remedy from the local drugstore. But when that person goes to the doctor and has a CT scan, a whole new level of understanding is possible. Similarly, the Holy Spirit is able not only to help us look deeper and see what's happening in our lives, but also to guide us in the process of healing.

When I read through the congregation's heart-shaped notes, I could tell that God was speaking to us about important aspects of our lives. I also realized that the notes contained nothing that had the capacity to bring long-term joy to a life. No one would later say, "The thing that really made life great was my lack of compassion and the way I lost my temper with my family." In many ways we know it's time to stop messing around, and yet often we feel power-less to eliminate the sin. We may hope for change, but by ourselves we make no real progress in the self-control department.

If you had a heart-shaped note and were going to write and tell God one thing you were sorry about in your life, what would it be? What would you confess? Now imagine your life without that issue in it. I'll bet that if suddenly it was gone, you would feel a weight fall off your shoulders. You would have less pain and guilt in your life. You would be more joyful. Others would enjoy being around you more. It would be a gift.

It's odd to imagine what our lives would be like without the mess that sin creates. Even when we think about just one sin, the impact could be significant. Consider a woman gazing at a social media site on her laptop. She looks at picture after picture of friends who seem so happy. Their children are smiling as they joyfully eat pomegranates and whole-grain snacks. There is not a potato chip in sight. Their husbands have surprised them with a special outing to celebrate their ten-and-a-half–year anniversary. They look fabulous in a new evening dress before a concert. They lost twenty pounds training for a marathon. As the woman views picture after picture, caption after caption, she feels smaller and smaller.

The sin taking root in her life is envy. The result is an almost overwhelming sense of inadequacy. Now consider what her day would be like if she would cooperate with God in removing this single sin. It would change the mental state she carries into every room she enters. It would affect the words she speaks to her children and the way she experiences the events of the day. She would be a better worker, leader, neighbor, and spouse. Most of all, she would dramatically improve her emotional health.

This evaluation and desire for change, however, is typically not the way we think about sin. Most of us have grown so accustomed to its presence that we no longer consider its outcomes. When we view sin as an inevitable part of our condition, more real to us than the image of God it obscures, we begin to accept as our fate not only the condition of sin but the effect of that particular sin in our lives. Over time, we lose our identity as being created in the image of God, believing in our corrupt nature and the despair it brings. At our worst, we lose hope.

The Cross

Justifying grace is the force that brings light and air to the aspects of our soul that have been closed up far too long. Not only do we need this initial realization that we have been deceived by sin; we also need power to break the hold it has over us. For Christians everywhere the symbol of that power is the cross of Jesus Christ.

Go anywhere in the world where Christians gather, and you will find a cross. It is mounted high on steeples, appears in elaborate mosaics, can be found in tiles on the floor or the wall of the sanctuary. Crosses appear in grottos and gardens and on the sides of roads and interstates. The tallest cross in the United States stands two hundred eight feet high in St. Augustine, Florida. The tallest cross in the world towers above the Valley of the Fallen in Spain. It is five hundred feet tall.[1] The cross is also worn by many of the faithful. For some it is small and simple, for others large and elaborate. It is on the cover of the Bible, the side of the pew, the bumper of a car, the pipes of the organ, and the forearm of the bass player.

For all its familiarity, however, there will always be something deeply mysterious about the cross. Why on earth would Christians regard a cruel instrument of execution as the sign of God's victory over sin in our lives? The reason is that the atonement or "at-one-ment" that Christ accomplished on the cross is so full of truth and power that it is simply not possible to express its meaning in just one way.

In the chapel of our church, there is an acrylic resin sculpture by Frederick Hart, titled the *Cross of the Millennium*.* The sculpture is a transparent cross, and inside is a figure of the Christ with his arms outstretched. It was Hart's desire to represent simultaneously the birth, death, and resurrection of Christ.[2]

---

* Hart was a well-known American sculptor whose Creation sculpture adorns the west façade of the Washington National Cathedral. His sculpture *The Three Soldiers* stands at the entrance to the Vietnam Memorial.

In the chapel, the cross is in a glass case that is lit from top and bottom, making the figure of Christ luminous. If you walk around the sculpture, you discover that the depiction of Christ is multifaceted: each angle of the cross exposes a slightly different perspective on Christ. In the same way, Jesus' death on the cross has a multitude of meanings that are helpful to us in different ways at different times in our lives.

From one angle, the cross simply reminds us that we are fallen and sinful human beings who are powerless to accomplish our own at-one-ment with God, for, after all, it is people like us who "crucified the Lord of glory" (1 Corinthians 2:8). From another angle, the cross proclaims the good news that "while we were still sinners" God accomplished what we could not (Romans 5:8). One familiar way of explaining how God does this is *penal substitution*, the idea that Jesus willingly bore the punishment for our sin that offends the holiness and righteousness of God. Protestant Reformers such as Luther and Calvin emphasized this view, as do many Christians today. Others, however, have put the emphasis in a slightly different place. Anselm of Canterbury held that Christ cancels our sins not by bearing our punishment, but by freely offering to God something that offsets the offense of sin—namely, his costly obedience on our behalf.

What the views of Luther, Calvin, and Anselm have in common is the idea that sin has consequences that must be dealt with. This is something that people often do not like to admit. But if you steal someone's car, you cannot simply say "I'm sorry" and think the matter settled. You have to return the car undamaged or compensate the owner for the value lost through your recklessness. If you spread rumors about someone that are not true, you can't just apologize. You have damaged their reputation through what you said. It is important that you go to those you spoke with earlier and tell them that you spread lies about the other person. It would be unjust for the person's reputation to be damaged while yours remained sterling, given that you spread the gossip and she or he did nothing wrong. Even after the apology was made and the story was put right, a sense of imbalance would remain. If the person took you to court and sued for defamation of character, the judge might require you to make some payment to the injured party. This would be a peace offering between the two of you. If the sum were reasonable, few would question why it had to be paid. The action has consequence. Another party was injured. The greater the damage experienced, the higher the penalty that must be paid.

On the cross God brings an end to
the imbalance that sin creates in our
relationships and the guilt we carry
for our actions. God does for us what
we cannot do for ourselves.

Many argue that it seems unjust for God to demand that Jesus die on the cross. This seems both unfair and illogical to them, given that Christians say God is love. But what a loving act, for the Father to send his own Son to offer reconciliation between humanity and its Creator. It is important to remember that it is God the Father, the Son, and the Holy Spirit who does this. The nature of the Trinity is such that we cannot separate the Creator from the Redeemer from the Sustainer. The Father is not an aloof Judge who demands justice and does not feel pain when the Son goes to the cross. On the cross God brings an end to the imbalance that sin creates in our relationships and the guilt we carry for our actions. God does for us what we cannot do for ourselves. God both recognizes the scope of human sin and makes an offering to bring peace between us. The death of Christ is a tangible act of mercy. The cross is not so much a symbol of pain and death as it is a symbol of love and grace. Here we see God's love, offered for the pardoning of our sin. Convinced of God's love, we follow the way of Christ joyfully, like children who feel they will be safe if they follow in their parents' footsteps. From this viewpoint the cross can be seen as a beautiful and costly gift. The gratitude we feel compels us to offer our lives as a gift to God in return.

This brings me to another view on the meaning of at-one-ment. Gazing at the *Cross of the Millennium,* I can see the resurrected Christ rise from his tomb with new life. Here Hart has captured another important way to think of what Christ accomplished through his crucifixion. On the cross, Jesus struggled against evil and the power of death, and, though he died, he never gave in. What is more, God the Father raised him from the dead so that he might offer new life to the world. This was not simply the offer of eternal life, but a willingness to liberate humanity from the grip of sin in the present moment. This theory of atonement, commonly called *Christus Victor*, or Christ the Victor, demonstrates both the willingness of God to do what humanity could not accomplish as well the power of the resurrection, which overcame death.

Gazing at the rising figure of Christ on the cross, I am reminded that we are powerless on our own. This is an essential admission if we hope to experience the restoration of God's image in this lifetime. Only with God will pride change into humility. Only with Christ will envy turn into admiration. Only with the Holy Spirit will the hatred of racism turn into the love of shared community.

Nicodemus's Questions

Nicodemus was a Pharisee and a respected leader in Jerusalem. He was well educated in the Law and well versed in its application. People came to him to find answers. But he had questions for Jesus, so he sneaked off to see him under the cover of darkness. We can picture Nicodemus looking left, right, and over his shoulder to see if he was being followed.

When he found Jesus, Nicodemus started out by saying he knew Jesus was of God because of all Jesus' miracles.

> *Jesus answered, "I assure you, unless someone is born anew, it's not possible to see God's kingdom."*
>
> (John 3:3)

Scholars agree that the original language can also be translated as "born from above" rather than "born anew" or "born again." Jesus wanted us to know that we must be born in a new way with the power of God's Spirit remaking our lives.

> *Nicodemus asked, "How is it possible for an adult to be born? It's impossible to enter the mother's womb for a second time and be born, isn't it?"*
>
> *Jesus answered, "I assure you, unless someone is born of water and the Spirit, it's not possible to enter God's kingdom."*
>
> (John 3:4-5)

Nicodemus seems to have found Jesus' words difficult to believe. As a law-abiding, rule-following, regulation-regarding, decree-dealing, directive-diligent Pharisee, what he probably found more difficult to believe was that he needed God's help to have the life Jesus described.

Jesus wanted Nicodemus to understand that without God's help, he never would experience the righteous life he was working so hard to achieve. It wasn't enough to know the answers; there were many ways to experience God. We read the moral law in the Hebrew Bible, compiled succinctly in the Ten Commandments. We feel the gentle leading of the Holy Spirit in our conscience. We see in the example of Christ one whose life is fully given over to the way of love. Our problem, in other words, is not a lack of information. As Mark Twain once said, "It ain't the parts of the Bible that I can't understand that bother me, it is the parts that I do understand."

New Birth

There's an important point to make about restoring God's image within us. We can't see God's grace as an endless well from which we draw buckets of mercy to ease our guilt about sins continually committed. The point of God's mercy is a transformed life, not a reset conscience. That is, God's goal is not for us to have less mess in our lives; it is to lift us out of our old life into a new one. The Lord wants nothing less than to give us a life that is full of meaning, deep satisfaction, and complete joy. There's nothing partial about it. It's not a matter of removing a layer or two of sin so that we can have a dim idea of what God's image looked like when it was fresh and new. To experience the intended level of change, we must become partners with God in the process of our restoration.

God's goal is not for us to have
less mess in our lives; it is to lift us
out of our old life into a new one.

When Jesus used the image of new birth, he reminded us that the process will be uncomfortable, even if it is a necessary starting point for our eventual growth to full maturity. I have seen each of our four daughters enter the world, and none emerged with a smile on her face. None of them looked around and said, "Thanks! What an enjoyable and invigorating process!"

Birth requires struggle, pain, pushing, rude awakenings, and entrance into an existence that is fundamentally different from the one we've grown used to. Babies would rather stay in the sheltered calm of their mother's womb than enter the uncertainty of a brightly lit world. Likewise, many of us wish that spiritual new birth meant you popped out like Athena, fully formed and wearing her armor. That is the myth. In real transformation, pain is part of the deal. Spiritual new birth is the starting point of all true growth, which will continue for a lifetime.

New birth can feel uncomfortable, because we are not just coming alive to Christ; we are dying to an old way of living. The experience of that death, even if our old life was not so great, will include grief for what it was and what it wasn't. But we must leave it. We must abandon that way of life if God is to bring us the new. Christ came for nothing less than the total transformation of our lives and total restoration of our souls.

One man, new to the Christian life, read a daily devotion based on the third chapter of James. He felt unusually convicted when he read,

> *People can tame and already have tamed every kind of animal, bird, reptile, and fish. No one can tame the tongue, though. It is a restless evil, full of deadly poison. With it we both bless the Lord and Father and curse human beings made in God's likeness. Blessing and cursing come from the same mouth. My brothers and sisters, it just shouldn't be this way!*
>
> (James 3:7-10)

Reading the Scripture, the man realized that as a Christ follower he would have to change his style of humor. Cutting sarcasm had to die. He also realized he had to change the way he spoke about others. Criticism had to die. He often spoke in a way that demonstrated contempt of people around him. Contempt had to die. These deaths would not be easy or enjoyable. Reading the Scripture, the man felt as if part of his personality was dying. But as he began walking in the way of Christ and following the guidance of the Holy Spirit, he allowed God to change the way he interacted with others. As a result, anyone who knew the man could see him becoming a new person.

The Apostle Paul tells us that such convictions and changes are possible through God's love:

> *God is rich in mercy. He brought us to life with Christ while we were dead as a result of those things that we did wrong. He did this because of the great love that he has for us. You are saved by God's grace!*
>
> (Ephesians 2:4-5)

Paul refers to the outcomes of this new way of living as the fruit of the Spirit, and he lists some of them in his Letter to the Galatians.

> *But the fruit of the Spirit is love, joy, peace, patience, kindness, goodness, faithfulness, gentleness, and self-control. There is no law against things like this. Those who belong to Christ Jesus have crucified the self with its passions and its desires. If we live by the Spirit, let's follow the Spirit.*
>
> (Galatians 5:22-25)

We observed that nothing the congregation wrote on those heart-shaped pieces of paper was going to bring anything other than sorrow; conversely, these fruits of the Spirit can only bring joy. Embracing new life in Christ means we have the potential to experience a joy that is deeper than our circumstances or any temporary emotion.

Sin brings us pain and even misery. If we allow it to create a mess, we will soon find our lives unnecessarily complicated and unhappy. But if, as Paul says, we "live by the Spirit" and "follow the Spirit," then our lives will produce fruit consistent with the season.

The question becomes how we sustain such a life over time.

The Vine

A vine is growing in my neighbor's yard. It overtook one of the bushes but has not been content to stop there. This vine is on a mission. From the top of the bush it is growing at a 45-degree angle toward a nearby tree. The tendril looks like an outstretched arm that's reaching to get something off the top shelf. I went over and stared at it. I could almost feel its desire to attach itself and keep growing. I wondered how it even knew that the tree was there. How could it tell where to grow?

I looked it up. The process is called *phototropism*. Plants have a hormone called *auxin* that enables them to grow toward sunlight so they'll be able to generate energy through photosynthesis. Somehow the vine knows that if it can attach itself to something higher, there will be more sunlight. More sunlight means more energy, so it grows toward light and heat.

At first I disliked the way that vine was taking over the bush and trying to cover the tree. Now I find that I admire this plant. I admire its struggle and its focus. It has nothing to cling to but reaches toward its goal nonetheless. I monitor its progress. My neighbor really should cut it back, but these days I'm sort of rooting for the vine.

When I see the vine, I feel God's Spirit asking me what I am growing toward, what I am straining for. I know that God has provided all the light and heat I need. I also know that without God's power, all my straining will get me nowhere. It makes me think of what Paul said in his Letter to the Philippians:

> *The righteousness that I have comes from knowing Christ, the power of his resurrection, and the participation in his sufferings. It includes being conformed to his death so that I may perhaps reach the goal of the resurrection of the dead.*

> *It's not that I have already reached this goal or have already been perfected, but I pursue it, so that I may grab hold of it because Christ grabbed hold of me for just this purpose. Brothers and sisters, I myself don't think I've reached it, but I do this one*

thing: I forget about the things behind me and reach out for the things ahead of me. The goal I pursue is the prize of God's upward call in Christ Jesus. So all of us who are spiritually mature should think this way, and if anyone thinks differently, God will reveal it to him or her. Only let's live in a way that is consistent with whatever level we have reached.

(Philippians 3:10-16)

There is a gap between the vine and the destination, much like the gap between Adam and God on the Sistine Chapel ceiling. Closing that gap fully is the work of a lifetime, and it is what we will talk about in the next chapter.

5

ADDRESS THIS MESS

Happy are the people whose strength is in You, whose hearts are set on pilgrimage.

(Psalm 84:5 HCSB)

When I was in high school I had a friend whose parents bought a dilapidated Victorian home that had been owned by two brothers. The two brothers had grown up in the house. Neither brother married, which seemed fairly understandable given how hard they found it to get along with each other. The brothers agreed to split down the middle all bills related to the home. The problem was that they could not agree on what upkeep the home needed.

Neither brother wanted to invest much in the house, so any good idea for maintenance raised by one brother was considered a bad idea by the other. Eventually they drew a line of demarcation at the center of the porch, and each agreed to pay for expenses related to his side of the house. If the problem happened on your side of the house, you paid for it.

This logic seemed to solve matters initially, but the brothers soon learned that a problem on one side of the house could bring dramatic issues to the other. Take the roof, for example. It needed repair in one section, which meant it needed repair in the other. But they could never agree on the contractor or materials, so the repair was never done. The complaining between the brothers never stopped, and the work on the roof never started.

All this is to say that by the time my friend's parents bought the Victorian, it was a mess. The roof was full of holes. The water damage was so severe that the attic floor had fallen into a second-story bedroom. The yard was overgrown. The front porch was dangerous. Only the fading memory of exterior paint remained.

On a few occasions I had the opportunity to help my friend and his dad do restoration work on this home. My favorite part was the first phase. We would enter a room and demolish the walls. Because of water damage, the lath and plaster would have to be removed. Using hammers, crowbars, and other tools perfectly suited to the interests and aptitudes of teenage boys, we tore the walls apart. It was loud, dirty, and destructive work. In many ways, the mess we were addressing got a lot messier before it got better. Everything had to go.

The second phase was the restoration of those walls. I never helped with that part of the process. It took skill, care, and vision that my good intentions could not supply. There was concern for the quality of the finished product. They wanted every room to look beautiful. Every step, from the drywall and plaster repair to the paint and wallpaper, was done with attention to detail. Over time, this family worked through the house room by room, removing what was damaged and restoring things to their original beauty. Their restoration effort was so complete and beautifully done that their Victorian was eventually included in our town's annual tour of homes. People were simply amazed at the transformation.

Sanctifying Grace

The transformation that God makes possible in our own lives takes place through *sanctifying grace*. Prevenient grace is God's work in our lives before we are aware of it; justifying grace seeks to show us who we are and where we fall short; and sanctifying grace works on us and with us to restore the image of God in our lives.

In a sense, sanctifying grace has both a negative and a positive effect. Just as things got worse before they got better at my friend's house, sanctifying grace can be difficult at first. In order to do the work of restoration, grace must continually identify character flaws that have been created by sin. Holes in the roof and shortcomings in our character must be exposed before they can be fixed. Luckily, that's not the end of the process. If it were, we would to be like a house where the roof was repaired and every room was down to the studs. God's desire is that we end up not just free of sin but perfected in love. While justifying grace identifies the project as a whole, sanctifying grace works in the details. It is essential for both the ongoing identification of what needs to be restored in our lives and the upbuilding work of God that enables us, over time, to grow and mature in our ability to share love.

God's desire is that we end up not just free of sin but perfected in love.

Jesus was clear about the ultimate goal of the process. When asked what the greatest commandment was in the Law, he responded,

> "You must love the Lord your God with all your heart, with all your being, *and with all your mind. This is the first and greatest commandment. And the second is like it:* You must love your neighbor as you love yourself. *All the Law and the Prophets depend on these two commands."*
>
> (Matthew 22:37-40)

The goal of the sanctified life is to express perfect love in every situation. It is a full transformation. The negative and positive aspects of sanctifying grace work together for this purpose. By dealing with our sin, God is able to set us free to enjoy the life for which we are intended. Every sin we commit is holding love hostage in some way. We need God's help to clear away that sin. We are like a seagull that becomes entwined in a plastic grocery bag while picking through a pile of garbage. A bird designed to fly, to skim the water, to hover in the air or move at great speed, is stuck on the ground. Its movement will remain hindered until someone intervenes.

We have the same problem. If Fred is jealous of Alexis because of the attention she receives for her work and the frequency of her promotions, he will not have the ability to hold her in the light of

Christian love. Jealousy can foster contempt and encourage him to assume the worst about Alexis. Fred will examine Alexis with critical eyes, always looking for evidence to justify his jealousy. Fred's jealousy is like the seagull's plastic bag. It holds Fred down.

We are in need of an outside force to strip away the encumbrance and set us free. The only way for love to emerge in Fred's work life is for God to do what Fred cannot. It's not enough for Fred to avoid jealousy; he must ask God to replace his tendency toward jealousy with an impulse to love. Perhaps this is why King David prayed,

> *Create a clean heart for me, God;*
> *   put a new, faithful spirit deep inside me!*
>
> (Psalm 51:10)

In Fred's case, he will need to ask God to help him release any grudges he holds against Alexis, recognize her contributions to their project team, and then express his appreciation for her in ways that specifically honor her work. This means that Fred will need to get to know Alexis. He will need to ask about the vocational background, education, and experience that inform her work. In so doing, Fred will be able to develop a genuine relationship with her and gratitude for her. As Fred allows God's love to direct him, he will not only overcome jealousy but replace it with a new experience of Alexis as a child of God. He will begin to see Alexis in the same way Jesus sees her. Rather than doling out contempt, he will begin to extend the same grace and pardon to Alexis that he knows Christ has extended to him.

The ability to see people in the light of God's love and mercy is the major difference between those who are full of Christ's love and those who are not. Those grateful for forgiveness are able to forgive. Those aware of their own imperfections understand the flaws that others display. Those who see the goodness of God in their own lives can readily affirm it in the lives of others.

Filled with Christ's love, we no longer feel angry or embittered toward others. We appreciate the fact that they have their own struggles, just as we do. We also realize that many of the frustrations we experience toward others are actually unresolved issues in our own lives.

The Power of Humility

Sanctifying grace works much faster in an environment of humility. This is why, in a twelve-step group, a person might introduce herself by saying, "I'm Angela, and I'm a _____." (Fill in the blank with your mess of choice.) Angela doesn't mind saying it, because she has lost the desire to live behind a façade or think more highly of herself than is warranted. She just wants to change. And if the pathway to change requires being honest about her flaws and her need for God's grace and power, so be it. She is all in, because she wants to get all out of her old life.

Humility is a slippery virtue. If we say we are working to become humble, we will undoubtedly begin to take pride in our progress, which will take us further from our goal. One might ask if it's even possible to develop our humility intentionally; maybe it's more a part of our nature than a quality nurtured over time.

But humility must be pursued. It's possibly the most important trait that Christ followers can cultivate in their lives. Humility takes the focus off ourselves. It helps us lay down our self-idolatry. It allows us to be concerned about the needs of others. Without humility, so much of our time is spent dwelling on injustices done to us or appreciation that was not offered. We seek the easy path and take great care to avoid discomfort, often at the expense of relationships that require attention or good works we could have done. Humility is the remedy for these behaviors. It allows us, by overcoming our idolatrous love of self, to focus on others and have both the time and energy to do so.

A few years ago, at a graduation speech at Wellesley High School in Massachusetts, English teacher David McCollough Jr. shocked students, parents, and faculty with his words to the graduates:

> You've been pampered, cosseted, doted upon, helmeted, bubble-wrapped.... You've been feted and fawned over and called sweetie pie.... But do not get the idea that you're anything special. Because you're not.[1]

McCullough pointed out that once we become convinced we are special, we will act in ways that serve ourselves, which will negatively change many things in our lives. He instead pointed students to what he called

> the great and curious truth of human experience...that selflessness is the best thing you can do for yourself. The sweetest joys of life, then, come only with the recognition that you're not special. Because everyone is.[2]

In other words, selflessness is only found in those who have made a turn toward humility—or, as McCullough put it, those who are able to recognize they are not as special as they once imagined.

Humility is connected to the desire to love God with our mind. It is a way of viewing our lives, and it requires us to control our thoughts about ourselves and others. We think we are kind, loving, forgiving, gracious, good drivers, pleasant, great conversationalists, empathetic, sympathetic, and even a bit telepathic. In our heart of hearts, most of us are fairly certain that if we were in charge of the government, school, dance studio, doctor's office, church, post office, soccer team, university, or grocery store, it would run more efficiently, effectively, pleasantly, graciously, and successfully. We think this because, deep down, most of us believe we are kind of special. Okay, really special.

Wouldn't it be great if the human body came equipped with gauges? Consider a young man who is buying an engagement ring. The young man feels love when he thinks of his future fiancée and assumes this makes him a loving person. He may, in fact, be a minor dictator to his parents and an undependable friend to his buddies, the kind of person who wouldn't change a flat tire for the elderly woman he sees alongside the highway. But he feels attraction, so he assumes he is full of love. Before he buys the engagement ring it would be great if he could look in a mirror to read a gauge on his forehead. The scale would run from *benevolent* to *blockhead*, and tell him if he would be a good husband. The system would be better still if his fiancée had one too. Because such self-evaluation is difficult, we must pursue humility.

The English word *humility* comes from the Latin *humilitas*, which can be translated as "lowness" or "submissiveness" and is derived from *humus* (earth).[3] A humble person, then, is well-grounded. Humility is a way of stabilizing and re-orienting one's life with God without taking multiple falls from the heights of pride to the valley of self-loathing. Humility has a way of gently removing the obstacles to the growth of love in our lives that inner pride and idolatry place there. It is a part of who we are, in the same way that the earth becomes a part of the plant. We don't need a dose of humility; we need humility to become our constant state of being.

Humility has a way of gently removing the obstacles to the growth of love in our lives that inner pride and idolatry place there.

Being humble is made more difficult because humility isn't necessarily a celebrated virtue in our culture. Some want to avoid humility because it feels like defeat or failure. Christians, however, understand that humility is a path not to defeat but to restoration.

It's useful to remember that there's a big difference between humility and humiliation. We can pursue humility, readily admit our failures and shortcomings, and realize we have work to do if we're going to be a more loving spouse, parent, worker, or friend. When humility is a part of our lives, we are far less likely to gossip about others, push them out so we can be the center of attention, speak when we should be silent, or hold prejudice toward others so we can feel superior to them. Humility will ground us in the ways of Christ.

Humiliation, by contrast, is most likely to occur when we lose humility. Humiliation comes when pride leads us to speak as if we have all knowledge, act as if we have all power, and judge others as though we are omniscient. All these experiences, and the embarrassment that can result, are an outcome of pride.

The key is to walk in the Lord's ways, making sure that God's presence is the place where we dwell. When we find humility, God promises to be there:

> *For thus says the high and lofty one*
> *who inhabits eternity, whose name is Holy:*
> *I dwell in the high and holy place,*
> *and also with those who are contrite and*
> *humble in spirit,*
> *to revive the spirit of the humble,*
> *and to revive the heart of the contrite.*
>
> (Isaiah 57:15 NRSV)

Humility is a journey, a path on which we see ourselves as we really are, with all our flaws, sins, and imperfections. Knowing who we really are enables us, with God's help, to see who we can become.

On the journey of humility, we see God's power for transformation, even as we realize the limits of our own. We long for God, knowing there is no progress on the journey without God's presence and power. We grow in sanctification, understanding that we can't prove ourselves righteous through good works. We see good works as an outcome or fruit of the Holy Spirit. Humility makes us too honest with ourselves to believe we can be perfectly righteous without God's help. We understand that what we do is not comparable to what God has done. Again and again, because of humility, we are reminded that our primary resources are the Lord's presence and the Lord's ways. This insight is expressed in the Book of Isaiah, when the Lord offers,

> *I have seen their ways, but I will heal them.*
> *I will guide them,*
> *and reward them with comfort.*
>
> (Isaiah 57:18)

Our participation in sanctifying grace is what produces a growing ability to love God and others. Humility is essential to this process, because it gets us out of sin's rut and allows us to remember with gratitude, not resentment, that God has better things in mind for us. In the words of Isaiah,

> *My plans aren't your plans,*
> *nor are your ways my ways, says the* Lord.

(Isaiah 55:8)

Spiritual Disciplines

Humility leads us to understand that in order to grow in love, we must give God's grace clear and unobstructed pathways into our lives. If these paths are open and well worn, the process of restoration will take place. For many people, those paths are spiritual disciplines.

Just as sound building practices enabled my friend and his family to rebuild the walls of their house, so spiritual disciplines bring proper techniques and attention to the restoration of our souls. Spiritual disciplines allow God to work within us and use our lives to bless others. Through these practices, the positive work of sanctification is done. These are ancient practices that Christians have found essential to their life in Christ for centuries. They are tried and true. They allow God to promote hope where there is despair, beauty instead of trivialized lust, gentleness over anger, respect of others in place of bigotry and racism, and a growing ability to love in all things.

Even while engaging in these disciplines, we must always remember that the work is being done through God's sanctifying grace. Richard Foster writes, "God freely and graciously invites us to participate in this transforming process. But not on our own."[4]

When we engage in the spiritual disciplines, we open ourselves up to God's presence. Spiritual disciplines are practices that enable us to receive God's presence and love. Dallas Willard suggests that the practices tend to fall into two categories. Disciplines of abstinence include solitude, silence, frugality, chastity, secrecy, and sacrifice. Disciplines of engagement include study, worship (here I would add the sacraments), celebration, service, prayer, fellowship, and confession.[5]

These practices are a gateway through which we can enjoy the presence of God's Spirit and the Risen Christ, and they have been used going back to biblical times. We can see them in the account of Jesus' visit to Mary and Martha. Hospitality was an important value in Jesus' culture. Since Jesus was a celebrated rabbi and close friend, Mary and Martha would have worked to make his visit special. They would have prepared a room for him to sleep and a special meal. Both sisters would have prepared diligently for his arrival.

Once he arrived, Mary sat down to listen to Jesus. Unlike virtually any other rabbi in Israel at that time, Jesus welcomed women who wanted to learn from him. We can imagine the conversation involving Jesus, Mary, and the other guests. This was the opportunity they had been waiting for. You too can spend time with Jesus, through spiritual disciplines.

Prayer

Consider the many ways God is able to speak to us through prayer. Prayer affords us the opportunity to slow down and consider our lives in the presence of God. When we pray, we have the chance to confess aspects of our lives that need change and ask for God's guidance. We seek God's wisdom for decisions that must be made and ask help for those in need.

> Through prayer we can go to God about our personal lives, about the people we love, and about the state of the world, reminding ourselves that God remains sovereign in the universe.

Through prayer we can go to God about our personal lives, about the people we love, and about the state of the world, reminding ourselves that God remains sovereign in the universe. Time with God in prayer is essential if we are to honor Jesus' teaching that "sufficient for the day is its own trouble" (Matthew 6:34 ESV). We must learn to trust God, but it can only be done if first we spend time with God. It's not possible, after all, to trust God if our habits keep God at a distance. Intimate conversation with God through the spiritual discipline of prayer enables us to enter the presence of the divine Spirit.

Silence

Sometimes words elude us, and the time we spend with God is in silence. This is a very difficult practice for most people. We have taught ourselves to multitask in most environments. Music plays while we drive our cars or do our homework. Incoming text messages ding in the background while we work on an important project. While talking with others, we are also looking at social media on our phones. People do e-mail while participating in conference calls, play podcasts while walking the dog, and watch videos while doing the dishes. Rarely do we do one thing at a time. Almost never do we stop, quiet our minds, enter silence, and just listen.

For some, the conditioning of multitasking is so strong that stillness produces an experience of restlessness that has to be overcome. Yet silence is a place where God uniquely seems to dwell. This may be why so many people find nature to be a sacred space. Throughout the Bible we are told to observe nature. The Psalms tell us that we will see God's handiwork in the sun, moon, and stars. God tells Job to consider the seas and rivers and their inhabitants, the whale and the crocodile. Jesus tells his followers to consider the lilies of the field.

I was fly fishing recently, and it occurred to me how long it had been since I had stood in a river and gazed at the flowing water, the majestic mountains beyond, and the gorgeous blue sky above. It had been too long since I had just stood still and heard nothing. The surroundings were so free of cars, airplanes, phones, and people that I was able to hear almost everything around me. The water babbling over rocks, the wind moving through tall grass, the faint swoosh of the fishing line as I cast—these small sounds worked to quiet my mind and reset my thoughts. And here is a fisherman's secret: I didn't care if I caught a fish. I just wanted the experience of a focused mind that was alive to the world. The experience right-sized me. It made me realize that God is big and I am small. I felt joyfully humble.

Nature is the most popular cathedral. When people say they feel close to God in nature, perhaps it isn't the visual environment that brings this experience; it may be the silence, in which we can allow our minds to be at rest. When we are silent before the ocean, quiet in a desert, or still at the summit of a trail, we make room for God's still, small voice to speak to us, guiding our thoughts to see people and circumstances in new ways.

Service

Another spiritual discipline that enables us to connect with God is service. In the church I serve, there is a woman named Franki who sends notes of encouragement. I have received several of these notes over the years. They often show remarkable timing. They arrive on a day when I can use a kind word or an expression of appreciation. Franki has a way of seeing things in me that I don't see in myself. I can imagine Franki sitting at her desk, thoughtfully considering her recipients. Whenever I read one of her notes, it's obvious she has been thinking about me, discerning what concerns me, where I need encouragement, or which words of appreciation will inspire me. In fact, her messages are so on-point that I often feel as though God is speaking to me through Franki.

I asked Franki how many notes she writes, and she replied, "Twenty or twenty-five a week. I write them every Sunday right after church." I asked her why she started writing them and she said, "I write a lot of notes at work, telling our clients how much I appreciate them. I thought it would be nice if I would do that for our church family. I thought it would be nice if people knew that I cared for them and loved them."

Each of her messages is only one small note, but it is a tangible expression of love. It seems no coincidence that Franki engages in this form of service after worship. She has celebrated God's presence and contemplated God's goodness. Having loved God, she then writes notes in which she expresses love of neighbor. I wonder what the world would look like if love could grow in each of us the way it exists in Franki. It would certainly be a boost to the U.S. Postal Service! But in addition to Franki's notes, I can also imagine the millions of other kind acts that would be offered if everyone cultivated love the way Franki does.

Learning from Mary and Martha

The goal here is not to review every spiritual discipline, but to emphasize that when we consistently engage in these practices, we discover that God is present for us. At Mary and Martha's house, the time Jesus spent with those who stopped, listened, and engaged in conversation showed God's desire to have a relationship with us. Our growth in sanctification occurs when our relational availability is as consistent as God's. In the account of Jesus' visit, Mary's devotion to Christ was exemplary. Martha, however, is the sister to whom many of us relate.

> *By contrast, Martha was preoccupied with getting everything ready for their meal. So Martha came to him and said, "Lord, don't you care that my sister has left me to prepare the table all by myself? Tell her to help me."*
>
> (Luke 10:40)

There was nothing wrong with the hospitality Martha wanted to offer. It was expected of her to provide a room for Jesus to stay and meals for him to eat. There were no shortcuts to food preparation in those days. If water was to be boiled, first a fire had to be built.

If bread was to be baked, flour had to be milled. The list of tasks to be accomplished when a guest arrived, especially a guest of Jesus' magnitude, would have been long. Martha wanted to get it right.

At the same time, though, we can see that something wasn't quite right. Martha was snippy with Mary about spending time with Jesus when there still were preparations to be made. She was confrontational with Jesus. She tried to blame Mary's serenity for her own anxiety. She wanted Jesus to believe that Mary didn't care about Martha's situation. In her words to Jesus, Martha tried to give shame to Mary and guilt to Jesus.

But while Martha was wondering why Mary was in the living room, Jesus was wondering why Martha was still in the kitchen.

> The Lord answered, "Martha, Martha, you are worried and distracted by many things. One thing is necessary. Mary has chosen the better part. It won't be taken away from her."
>
> (Luke 10:41-42)

Christ wants us, like Martha, to understand that we need to find time with him amid the competing claims of our family, friends, home, vocation, and larger community. We live in a time when there are more ways than ever to increase our time with God. We can read the Bible on a mobile device. Online services can send us daily reading plans to keep the Scripture before us in organized ways. The writings of great saints from every era are found in books or through a brief Internet search. The issue is not access; it is the discipline to seek out fresh experiences of God's presence.

One reason we spend time with God is to understand and communicate what's going on in our lives. Remember that the next time you have a moment like the one Martha had. We speak sharply. We make demands readily. We see injustice all around us. Pausing to be with Christ quickly reveals that our lives are in balance with our culture but out of balance with God's reign. That balance can be restored through the regular practice of spiritual disciplines.

Notice that Jesus does not criticize Martha's actions; he diagnoses her soul. We are told that Martha is distracted. In Greek, the word is *perispao*. It has the sense of being pulled in many directions at once. You've been there, haven't you? The responsibilities of the day all gang up on you and demand attention. The outer life tells you there's no time or energy for the inner life; doing overcomes being. It's spiritual death by multitasking.

The next time you get over-the-top busy and start being short with people, tell them you're suffering from a bout of *perispao*. They might say, "I think they sell something for that down at the drugstore. I can't remember if it's a pill or cream." And you'll say, "No, this is something different."

Perispao describes our inner life when we are anxious over what's happening around us. It involves being diverted from our lives with God because we're so energetically fulfilling our roles and responsibilities. In attempting to get everything right, we forget or avoid God's gracious presence. Distracted from Christ, we enter a downward cycle into the mess. Suddenly we say things we regret and do things we shouldn't. In trying to clean up the old mess, we make a new one.

We are distracted. Jesus tells us that just one thing is needed: time with him. That's why you and I need spiritual disciplines. The world never recalled what Martha served for dinner, but we all remember Jesus' message that Mary made the wiser choice.

Spiritual disciplines allow us to receive the Spirit of God in prayer and study. We listen for God's voice in silence, exalt God's Spirit in worship, and engage in practices that enable God to do the negative and positive work of sanctification. These practices are vital to the Christian life. They are as crucial to life in Christ as inhaling and exhaling are to breathing.

Sometimes our lives are like a strenuous hike in high altitudes, where the oxygen content is low. How often do you take time to deeply breathe in the air of God's Spirit? It's worth noting that the first word used for God in Genesis 1 is *Ruach*, a Hebrew term meaning the air, wind, or Spirit of God. Spiritual practices enable us to take in the breath of heaven and find renewal as a result.

Author and preacher Tom Long captures this in a story about a friend who accompanied a church youth group on a mission trip to Jamaica, where they met an exceptional teacher. They were surprised to hear her say, "Oh, I don't come here every day mainly because I love teaching. I come here every day because I love Jesus, and I see Jesus in every one of these children."

Long continues, "I think that teacher had been like Mary, sitting at Jesus' feet. And because she had, she could get up like Martha and teach those children with joy and hope, seeing Jesus in the face of every one of them."[6]

Think of how many significant things in your life would become easier if you were in the flow of God's love and grace. Consider how much less mess would be generated if you made time to sit with Jesus each day. Imagine what your life might become if you breathed the oxygen of God's presence, allowing it to infuse your life with goodness and God's sanctifying grace.

6

THE MESSAGE IN THE MESS

I'm sure about this: the one who started a good work in you will stay with you to complete the job by the day of Christ Jesus.

(Philippians 1:6)

If there is any message from God in the mess of life, it is this: You are deeply loved, and with God's help you can have and become so much more than you are right now.

As you've seen, in discussing sanctification we often use the metaphor of a journey or a path through life. The idea is that the further we travel along the path, the more we allow grace to work within us and the more like Christ we become. The goal of the journey is full sanctification, becoming so available to the grace and love of God in our lives that we respond to situations and circumstances the way Christ would.

This doesn't mean we lose our freedom and become like marionettes, pulled this way and that by strings from the Holy Spirit; or like avatars, directed by a divine keyboard in a cosmic game of *The Sims*. The idea of full sanctification is that our will is so formed in the love of Christ that sin no longer has the power to bring its mess to our doors. At the same time, love flourishes and enables us to bring great care and joy to others.

Getting Serious About the Message

In Colossians 3:1-17, the Apostle Paul portrays a life given over to the transformative power of God's grace. Paul first talks about the destructive power that sin brings to our lives. In a few verses he speaks of the sins people are most likely to find present in their lives: sexual immorality, covetousness, anger, the destructive use of speech, and lying. Paul writes, "You used to live this way, when you were alive to these things. But now set aside these things" (Colossians 3:7-8).

At this point, you might ask, "But Paul, does it all have to go? Couldn't we just enjoy a touch of envy, an occasional fit of anger, and perhaps a teeny bit of lust? And couldn't we still swear when we're out with our buddies, and swap a word or two of gossip among friends?"

Paul is having none of it. He gives you one of those raised-eyebrow looks and slowly says, "Put. It. To. Death."

This seems both clear and slightly intimidating. Then Paul turns quickly to the topic that really interests him. He tells you about your new life in Christ. This is not the life you instantly get when you realize that your life is a mess. You don't climb out of the mess all in one moment, like landing on the space in *Chutes and Ladders* that takes you all the way to the top. Yes, Jesus is the answer to your mess, but there is no shortcut to transformation. Paul tells you to take on the ways of Christ so you can change:

> *Therefore, as God's choice, holy and loved, put on compassion, kindness, humility, gentleness, and patience. Be tolerant with each other and, if someone has a complaint against anyone, forgive each other. As the Lord forgave you, so also forgive each other. And over all these things put on love, which is the perfect bond of unity. The peace of Christ must control your hearts—a peace into which you were called in one body. And be thankful people. The word of Christ must live in you richly. Teach and warn each other with all wisdom by singing psalms, hymns, and spiritual songs. Sing to God with gratitude in your hearts. Whatever you do, whether in speech or action, do it all in the name of the Lord Jesus and give thanks to God the Father through him.*
>
> (Colossians 3:12-17)

Reading these words, you realize that the life Paul describes is better than any part of life you have experienced. It is so great that you think it must be absolutely unachievable. It sounds too good to be true—for you, anyway. You are a person who has tidied messes, but you have never really been successful at eliminating the mess of sin. Here Paul is not just talking about avoiding lying or not thinking angry thoughts about others or not holding grudges. He is telling you that you are to become completely kind, forgiving, at peace, and defined by love.

You remember feeling like that once, when you were younger, on a weekend retreat. You recall being a really fine person that weekend, and the sense of love you felt was both sincere and palpable. But you had to go home. And by Wednesday you could feel your old life creep back in and that deep love that Christ put on you like a royal robe just slip away.

Paul isn't talking about just one weekend; he means your whole life. He says you can experience and offer God's love twenty-four hours a day, seven days a week, fifty-two weeks a year. So you say, "I don't know, Paul. That sounds like a lot more than I can pull off."

Paul gives you a sober but sympathetic look and repeats some things you may have missed: "The peace of Christ must control your heart.... The word of Christ must live in you richly.... Whatever you do, whether in speech or action, do it all in the name of the Lord Jesus and give thanks to God the Father through him" (Colossians 3:15-17).

That's when you realize that Paul really is serious. He thinks your life shouldn't just be patched up; it should be fully restored. That's why he calls it your new life. He wants you to understand that the gap between you and the Almighty can be closed, but only if you cooperate with God's work in your life. Paul, amazed at what God can do, says you can have a life of such beauty that people will see the image of God in you. Parents, siblings, spouse, children, friends, neighbors, the homeless woman in the park, the umpire at the baseball game, the woman who waits on you at the DMV—all of them will smile when they see you, because there's something about your new life that does that to people.

> Jesus' death and resurrection happened
> for nothing less than the sanctification
> of all who would follow him.

Right now you may be thinking, *This book must be for other people. He can't be talking about me.* But the Bible's message is that Jesus' death and resurrection happened for nothing less than the sanctification of all who would follow him. Sanctification, complete sanctification, in which you are fully formed and owned by God's love, will reveal that you are in fact a masterpiece.

Love Divine, All Loves Excelling

Sometimes I think we have no idea what we're saying when we sing Charles Wesley's classic hymn "Love Divine, All Loves Excelling." The first stanza sounds so tame:

> Love divine, all loves excelling, joy of heaven, to
>   earth come down;
> fix in us thy humble dwelling; all thy faithful
>   mercies crown![1]

Who doesn't want to be a humble dwelling for Christ's love in the world? So we say, "Come on in, Lord, I have a room all prepared for you!" What we forget is that if Christ is going to enter the humble dwelling of one's life, he won't be there to take a nap; he will get to work. The carpenter's box he carried through your front door contains an assortment of tools. There's a putty knife, paintbrush, and roller, but before touching those he will be using a crowbar, hammer, power drill, and, if necessary, a pickax. We should be aware of what we're getting into before singing the final stanza:

> Finish, then, thy new creation; pure and spotless
> let us be.
> Let us see thy great salvation perfectly restored
> in thee....

Perfectly restored? Do you understand what you're asking for here? When God was reaching out to Adam in Michelangelo's painting, this is what the Almighty had in mind. No wonder Adam barely reached back. Perfect restoration takes time and a lot of cooperative effort. The Christian life is not like one of those one-week total-home-renovation shows. It's an act of deep commitment over the course of a lifetime, with a lot of dust and inconvenience along the way.

I recall returning from college on break and finding the home where I grew up to be a total disaster. My parents were literally moving the kitchen from one room to another. Walls were down. Floors were missing. A plastic sheet was hung to contain dust and grime, and it wasn't working. My mom looked a little frazzled. Things crunched underfoot as we walked through the living room. Noticeably absent was the smell of fresh bread, a homemade pie, or the cookies she often baked for us when we came home.

I asked hopefully, "What's for dinner, Mom?"

She led me into the laundry room, where I found the only kitchen appliance left, a microwave oven. "Whatever can be cooked in that, son," she answered.

Ultimately the home renovation was worth it. But living through the process was tough. Maybe that's why Christians sometimes object to the concept of full or entire sanctification, which is also called *Christian perfection.*

"How can I be perfect?" they lament. "I'll never reach that point."

And they won't, by themselves. What they forget is that sanctification happens through God's grace.

What's the Alternative?

Nadeem showed up at Floris United Methodist Church on a cold Sunday morning in December 2011. He was smiling when I met him at the front door. I can't recall the exact conversation we shared that morning, but I remember the essential facts.

Nadeem was a Christian from Pakistan. Married with three children, he recently had left his country. It seemed that because he had shared his faith in Christ with an employee of his business, extremists had first harassed him and later threatened his life. Nadeem had fled to Canada, then had come to the United States, where for two months he had been held in a detention center by U.S. Immigration and Customs Enforcement while his case for asylum was verified. He had been released and now was in the United States with few friends, no family, and no way to earn an income. But he was alive, and that was no small blessing.

Over the years since I first met Nadeem, God has found many ways to bless his life. He entered seminary through scholarships. He found work as his immigration status allowed. He became an associate pastor on our church staff. He was able to bring his wife and children to make a new life in the United States.

Nadeem is grateful for all these things, but while much has been gained, much also has been lost. Nadeem cannot see the members of his family who are still in Pakistan. He has read news of churches that have been burned by extremists there. He has connections in towns where Christians have been murdered.

Recently one of our pastors was preaching a sermon on Jesus' teaching, "But I tell you, love your enemies and pray for those who persecute you" (Matthew 5:44 NIV). We were discussing this text together when the pastor turned to Nadeem and asked, "How do you do that? How do you love the people who took away so much of what you had?"

Nadeem paused thoughtfully and then replied, "What's the alternative? If I choose not to love my enemies, what am I choosing instead? Bitterness? Revenge? Rage? Do any of these look good to you?"

Rarely had I heard the gloomy alternatives to ignoring Jesus' teaching summed up so quickly. Nadeem certainly is not reconciled to those who persecuted him for his faith. But he is free of hatred and anger. He has chosen the path of Christ's love, and in so doing, he has released the toxins of anger and hate.

The journey to full sanctification is challenging. Most of us understand that much of our life journey feels like two steps forward, one step back. Sometimes it's two steps back and one step forward, or even one step back and fall off a cliff.

Paul's encouragement to experience *full restoration* is helpful here. We restore a car one system at a time, understanding that improvement in one is needed for the functioning of all. We restore a house one room at a time, knowing that if the job takes a really long time we may have to go back to a restored room and give it another coat of paint or a new carpet. After all, people live in this space while the restoration occurs. Life happens.

If we're intimidated by the idea of full restoration, what are our other options? What percentage of God's image would we choose? Do we want 25 percent of God's love? Would 42 percent be enough? Or 61 percent? Does 78 percent sound too lofty? And if we are 78 percent sanctified, what would be in the unsanctified, unloving 22 percent of our souls? Would one person get that unsanctified part of us, or would we let everyone enjoy that equally?

When people tell me that we shouldn't expect to be sanctified in this lifetime or, worse yet, that salvation is just about getting into heaven and little more, I wonder why they would settle for so little when God wants to give them so much. Is that really what we're striving for—an acceptable level of greed, just a bit of lust, or a residual zone of bigotry?

When we aspire to the full restoration made possible through God's sanctifying grace, we find that the more we long for God's love to live in us, the more unacceptable the distortion of sin becomes. Here is the truth about our lives: we cannot honor sin and the presence of God in the same moment. As Jesus said, "If a house is divided against itself, that house cannot stand" (Mark 3:25 NIV).

But sin is ever at work. Evil does not have the power of God, but the temptations it generates can certainly appeal to humans. This is why, even as we strive for full sanctification, we find the mess creeping back into our lives.

The Problem of Entropy

Reading through the works of the church's great saints, one sees a common element arise: at some point, most of them have a crisis of faith. That leads us to a term I've borrowed from thermodynamics: entropy.

The idea is that systems lose energy over time, and things move from order to disorder. Think about your garage or basement. Ever notice how a few weeks after you spent all day cleaning up, it starts returning to its former state? Consider relationships. How is it that deep appreciation and shared love can devolve into anger and an inability to communicate?

Entropy doesn't just apply to our physical and emotional lives; it's at work in our spiritual lives as well.

Entropy doesn't just apply to our physical and emotional lives; it's at work in our spiritual lives as well. A once-exciting journey of personal healing and restoration becomes a lackluster routine of uninspired worship, unfocused prayer, sporadic Bible study, and a sense of spiritual dryness. We come to feel that the experience of God we once had was not real. It's surprising how quickly it can happen. The habits of love suddenly feel high-maintenance. Sin becomes unusually attractive.

Some call this experience backsliding, and indeed the term fits if we think of our spiritual life as a linear journey from one point to another. We stop pursuing the ways of God. We are no longer growing in love, and soon we are sliding backward.

I like the concept of entropy better, because when my spiritual health starts to fade, it feels more like a systemwide problem. I'm not returning to a prior state; I'm coming undone in every area.

The poet William Butler Yeats, in his poem "The Second Coming," reflected on the state of humanity during the horror of

World War I. Yeats was describing something more far-reaching and profound than an individual experience of slipping away from God, but the dynamic is the same.

> Turning and turning in the widening gyre
> The falcon cannot hear the falconer;
> Things fall apart; the centre cannot hold....

When I no longer hear the voice of the Holy Spirit guiding my life, things fall apart.

The Importance of Continual Engagement

A young woman I know suffered a crisis of faith and showed great creativity in dealing with it. I have known Anna since she was a child and have observed that as she has moved through various seasons of her life, her faith in Christ has always been important to her. When she went off to college, she found a campus ministry where she participated in a small group, served those in need, and attended retreats and events that helped her continue to mature as a follower of Christ.

During college, Anna went to France as an exchange student. I was somewhat surprised to hear that her experience studying abroad was a real challenge to her faith. I asked Anna to write about her experience. Here is what she shared:

> It was about week three when I noticed it. I wasn't acting like myself anymore. I became hyperconscious about my appearance, started doubting the sincerity of my friends and host family, came to quick judgments about new friends, and completely lost my sense of grounded wholeness. I'm sure you've heard the phrase "trash

in, trash out." Well, I believe the opposite is true as well. "Goodness in, goodness out." I was in a new place with new people, a new routine, and even a new language. Studying abroad for a semester doesn't seem as daunting when it's advertised at orientation with quick anecdotes and freshly printed brochures. But there I was, in France, without the places or people that keep me in line with my spiritual practices. When I stopped my spiritual disciplines, I restricted the goodness inflow and consequently the potential goodness outflow. I had to improvise.

I started being more intentional with my people back home. Every eight days my sister would have one day off from her summer job as a camp counselor. Knowing we had a limited time to talk we would start our conversations with questions like "What is God teaching you?" and "How is your soul?" This time was sacred for us and was exactly what I needed. Additionally, my boyfriend was trying to get back into the discipline of reading his Bible every day. Even though at times I felt isolated and alone, knowing there were other people on this journey with me was indescribably comforting and encouraging.

I also created time and space for God again. I set my alarm for fifteen minutes earlier every morning so that I could spend time reading my Bible and praying. Instead of listening to music that objectifies women and idolizes relationships, I started listening to Christian music on my bus rides. I even turned my exercise time into a sort of spiritual practice to connect with God. Within a week or two, I found my footing and recognized myself again. And isn't that the most amazing part about God? We come, we go, we grow closer, we forget, we come back, and through it all God is constant, patient, forgiving, and waiting with arms open wide.

Assurance

One way to know if you are pursuing full restoration is the lack of anxiety you will feel in the process. Sanctifying grace brings a sense of assurance to us that is in unique contrast to the worry and disquiet generated when we lived by our own power and cherished our own pursuits. Assurance is a new way of seeing the work of God in our lives and in the world.

On a trip to Sierra Leone, Africa, I was in a small team that included two doctors and a nurse. We were being given a tour of Kissy Hospital, a United Methodist health facility that included an eye clinic. We entered the surgical area of the hospital, and the doctor conducting the tour said, "We are getting this area ready for cataract surgery. The woman we passed in the hall is nearly blind from cataracts, and the doctor will remove them in just a few minutes. Would you like to stay and observe?"

Before I could say, "Are you crazy? Absolutely not!" and run screaming from the room, the doctors and the nurse in unison all said, "We'd love to!"

A short time later, we watched the doctor remove the cataracts from the patient's eyes. It was fascinating. But what I remember most about the experience is what happened afterward. Sometime after the surgery was completed, we saw the woman again. She told us that for the first time in years she could see the color of the sky and the faces of people around her. She could not wait to see her children and grandchildren. She was absolutely aware of everything in a new way. I recall thinking how great it was that the church was still helping the blind to see, just as Jesus did.

God's grace enables us to see what God is doing in the world, and how we can be a greater part of it.

When sanctifying grace is active in our lives, it removes the spiritual cataracts that keep us from seeing God's presence around us. God's grace enables us to see what God is doing in the world, and how we can be a greater part of it. Here are some ways that Christians experience the assurance of our salvation and know that sanctifying grace is transforming us.

We trust in God's love.

When we were making the small-group videos that accompany this book, a group of us were brainstorming ideas, trying to find a good image that would communicate how important it is to trust God fully. The journey of faith begins with a leap of faith. Along the way, that level of trust will be an essential means through which the believer responds to God's love and grace.

During the discussion I said, "It reminds me of the tandem jump my daughter recently made. They hook you on to an instructor who carries the parachute, and my daughter told me there's a moment when you realize you have to trust the instructor completely because you are going to jump out of an airplane with that person. It's the ultimate leap of faith. We should get someone to do that."

Everyone liked the idea and thought it communicated the point well. Then there was silence as we considered who would do it. Finally I piped up and said, "You know, if I'm narrating the video, talking about trust, I can't really interview someone else. To do this right, I need to be the one to jump out of the plane."

And that's how I found myself in an airplane a few weeks later, preparing to jump.

It didn't require any expertise on my part. The instructor would do the real work. Hundreds of people around the world safely do this every day. I had told myself these things over and over again in the weeks before the day arrived.

Friends of mine have watched that video. Those who know me well say there are two moments when they can see something clearly on my face just before the jump. That something is fear. The first time is when the instructor tells me to move toward the open door on the side of the plane. The second is just before we jump. The look on my face at that moment seems to communicate something like *Please God, take me to heaven before they make me jump out of this airplane!*

Then we jump. The jump is fantastic. It is exciting and the view is beautiful and the freedom of falling through the air is exhilarating. The truth is that in spite of my fear, I trusted the instructor. I trusted his training, his experience, and the equipment he was using.

People who have assurance of their faith trust God the same way. We have fears but believe that God loves us. Think about how audacious it is to believe that God loves you. It's one thing to believe that God loves the world generally, the way you might love a sunset or a baseball team. But to believe that God loves you individually, the way you love a child or a grandchild or your niece or nephew—that takes a lot of boldness. And that's a kind of love that requires deep trust.

Maybe you have this assurance of God's love. Or maybe you are new and still a bit uncertain. If so, you may fear the leaps of faith required by the Christian life—leaps when we are forgiven, corrected by the Holy Spirit, cajoled to use our gifts in new ways, offered opportunities to love others, or told that one day we will dwell in heaven with God and the communion of saints. You know that sanctifying grace is at work in your life when you experience these leaps with a sense of mild trepidation but sufficient trust to allow you to step out into the unknown, believing that God is with you.

As Paul said, "If God is for us, who can be against us?" (Romans 8:31 NIV).

We are confident in God's ability.

Sitting at the beach, half-reading a book, I noticed a boy with a kite. I could see that he really wanted to fly that kite. He wanted that kite way up in the sky. I'm no expert, but I've flown a lot of kites over the years, and it looked to me as if it wasn't going to work. The sea grass was still. There wasn't a whisper of a breeze.

In spite of the conditions, the boy took off running down the beach with the kite trailing behind him. When he was moving fast enough, the kite would go up maybe two or three feet. He would let out line, and the kite would go higher. He ran faster. Eventually he would slow down, and the kite would plop to the ground, right back on the sand. He repeated this for the better part of half an hour, until finally he got so frustrated that he just sat in the sand and whined.

I didn't say anything. You don't want to be the strange man talking to kids on the beach. But I wanted to say, "Brother, I know how you feel."

It's a shame that he wasn't old enough to drive to the sand dunes just a few miles down the road. The wind blows there most of the time. He could have learned a valuable lesson: you have to give up trying to be the wind. You have to go where the wind is found.

So much of the Christian life is learning to position ourselves in the flow of God's Spirit. We don't control the Spirit, but we can control whether our kite is aloft in its stream. This effort requires confidence that the ways of God are better than our ways. We must reach the conclusion that doing life on our own is exhausting, and in the end unfulfilling, when compared to living in concert with the power of the Holy Spirit. We must be assured that trust in God will lead us to do things that don't occur to us readily and are hard to do, and doing them will have great benefit to our lives.

If trust is about believing that
God loves us, then confidence is
about realizing that God's ways are
simply better than our ways.

If trust is about believing that God loves us, then confidence is about realizing that God's ways are simply better than our ways. Free from the influence of sin and evil, God's will is for us to experience good things. We can do so through faith in God's love and the spiritual disciplines that provide pathways for God's grace in our lives.

We believe in God's future.

Assurance of salvation is primarily about the present, but it also informs our ability to trust the teaching of Christ about eternal life. Death is a predictable part of life and strikes at the core of the human experience. The death of a person we love dearly helps us to understand what we really believe about life, death, eternal life, and the existence of God's love and mercy.

Some believe that when the biological end of life occurs, there is nothing more. I have been with people who strongly held this view until someone dear to them died. Unexpectedly, they found themselves wondering about life after death. It wasn't a sudden bout of wishful thinking; it was that death had made them fully appreciate the goodness and beauty of the life that had been so beloved to them. They found it hard to believe that such a life could simply cease. Presented with an actual loss rather than the existential concept of death, resurrection and eternal life seemed possible for the first time.

Christians carry the assurance of eternal life as a deeply ingrained belief that overcomes the fear so many people feel about their death. When Christians face death, they do some very complicated emotional and spiritual work.

On one hand, they have to entrust those they love to God's enfolding grace. They must place their family members and others who depend on them under God's care. Only by entrusting these persons to God's provision can they peacefully leave.

At the same time, they have to entrust themselves to God's mercy and the provision of God in eternal life. No one can embark upon the great journey of death and resurrection without some sense of trepidation. It's the reason I had that odd look on my face right before I jumped out of the airplane. Sure, I was connected to someone I trusted. But I was also jumping into thin air. I had never done it before. When we face our own death, assurance allows us to experience the mixed emotions of apprehension and faith in God in such a way that "the peace of God that exceeds all understanding will keep your hearts and minds safe in Christ Jesus" (Philippians 4:7).

When we have this assurance, death is a sacred and holy experience. I recall feeling prompted by God to call the husband of a woman who was in hospice care. He told me how grateful he was for the call. His wife was in the last hours of her life. I drove over to be with them. About thirty minutes after I arrived, she was breathing her last breaths. I called her husband and son over, and with a friend of theirs we joined hands and prayed. I thanked God for her life, for the love of her marriage, for the mother she was to her son, and for the friendships she enjoyed. We offered thanks for the people she had blessed in her vocation, for her good mind and kind heart. As I prayed, I looked at the woman and her family. I felt that only a thin sliver of a veil separated earth and heaven. In such moments, the presence of God seems almost tangible.

There is so much more to this life than what we can own or earn or possess. There is so much goodness and beauty and transcendence. The sacred envelops us. The love of God swirls around us and empowers us. We can see the infinite value of every life, enabling us to experience the fullness of love with God and with one another. Assurance is the work of sanctifying grace, and it is God's desire to complete this work in us so we will be fully loving and in full union with Christ.

We believe we can be perfected in love.

Full sanctification is about so much more than our own personal experience of this life. It is about becoming the blessing that God enables us to be in our community and world. When people love God and conspire with God's grace against sin, they can have a profound impact on others. The vast majority of faithful Christ-followers won't be remembered by history, but their impact on the world should never be underestimated.

The more we love God, the more we become aware of daily opportunities to share that love.

The more we love God, the more we become aware of daily opportunities to share that love. Our love for God will affect the way we treat the environment and take care of all that God has created. We will feel concern toward people in distress, who may live half a world away but with whom we sense a connection of shared humanity. Our capacity to care for those we love will grow substantially, and we will become a model for others around us.

Thinking about it reminds me of an e-mail I received recently:

> A couple of weeks ago when I got to the fabric store where I work, I took over for one of my

co-workers, as it was time for her to go. She had been helping a couple who were there with their ninety-four-year-old father. They were helping him pick out fleece and load it up in their van. They were buying entire bolts of what we had. I asked what they were doing with all that fleece. I learned that the old gentleman made blankets for children in third-world countries. As of a couple of weeks ago, he had made over 6,500 blankets. When he wasn't sewing, he took care of his wife of seventy years who had Alzheimer's. I rang up the sale, and after giving them every discount and coupon I could find, they spent over eight hundred dollars.

The gentleman was in great shape and very quiet and thoughtful. He just smiled. His daughter and son-in-law were the ones doing all the talking. I wondered how many children's lives he had touched and warmed by being so generous and selfless.

When I saw that e-mail, it occurred to me that I might be reading about someone who had been perfected in love in this lifetime. I'm certain that if God is going to do that work in my life, it will take at least ninety-four years. It makes me grateful that the Lord is both patient and diligent. What would it be like for a person to love his wife and the world so deeply that he would do such things every day?

Think of the life that God is offering you. No fears. No regrets. Just love. Love. Love.

Restoring Our Souls

Around the time I was completing this manuscript, I was on an airplane taking off from Denver. It was an hour or so before dusk. As the plane gained altitude, I could see farms below. There were dark green circles of cultivated crops, and tractors in the wheat fields with large combines. I had been hoping to see the majestic Rocky Mountains, but the view was obscured by dark clouds and a slowly setting sun.

As the plane rose, we entered a cloudbank and all visibility was lost. Several seconds passed, and the color of the clouds intensified. Suddenly we popped through the clouds and began to fly slightly above them. There were white clouds that looked like big balls of cotton. On the tops of each, the sun created highlights of blue and purple.

I've flown many times and am familiar with the beauty of cloud formations. But there was something mesmerizing about the formations we passed through that day. Rarely had I seen anything quite so beautiful from the seat of a plane. The plane lifted above the clouds and flew west, chasing daylight. The sun continued to shine on the clouds as far as the eye could see. I know it's not accurate to imagine God above and humans down below, but that day it was hard not to feel that I had gained a divine perspective.

What struck me more than anything was that a God who loves extraordinary beauty has blessed us with such scenes. The Creator's desire is not just to have such things in the natural world, but to restore our souls and enable us to express our love so that others will see the majesty of God in our lives as well. To be fully restored means that the light of God's love flows through us as it did through those clouds. The power of the Holy Spirit illuminates our goodness, enables us to see the handiwork of our Creator in one another, and fills us with a sense of wonder at what God is doing in our world.

This is the worthy life that can be yours in Christ.

ACKNOWLEDGMENTS

Writing a book is a shared project in many ways, from the patience people show while things are coming together to the conversations that influence the content. My wife, Karen, took time to hear my ideas and read over initial drafts of the book. As a committed Christian and small-group leader, she has studied the Bible thoroughly and knows the ways of Christ. Her insights and affirmations have been valuable. The encouragement she provided to help her less-disciplined husband sit down and write has been indispensable. Our daughters, Rebekah, Kathryn, Hannah, and Sarah, also provided occasional accountability in this regard. Life is a group effort.

Years ago, leaders at Floris United Methodist Church encouraged me to speak, write books, and develop curriculum so that our ministry could be helpful to others. They are a generous congregation who embolden their pastor to think that what we have learned together might be useful to the larger church. Their encouragement to take the necessary time involved in these projects has been a blessing to me. I am grateful to have walked in the footsteps of Paul with a group from Floris, where I was able to see Michelangelo's *The Creation of Adam* in person. The study I did for that trip, along with the dialogue we enjoyed while traveling, brought Paul's words to life in a fresh way.

My colleagues on the Floris staff, especially Pam Piester, Tim Ward, Barbara Miner, Nadeem Khokhar, Bill Gray, and Jake McGlothin, worked with this material when it originally was a sermon series during Lent. They were helpful in their willingness to engage in dialogue about the nature of the Christian life. I am grateful to Pam Borland, my administrative assistant, for organizing time so that I could produce the manuscript. I appreciate Pam's ability to manage the calendar in ways that enabled me to be a pastor and author, and I am grateful for her willingness to look over the final draft.

Charlie Kendall and Justin Lucas at Moonbounce Media not only thought it was a good idea for me to jump out of an airplane for the cause, they also produced great videos for small groups. They greatly assisted in developing the concepts in this book through their conversation and unrelenting determination to talk and work until ideas communicated easily.

I am grateful to Anna Lopynski for sharing her insights with me. Dr. Steve Hoskins was kind to read through some chapters and offer his insights. Who knew, when I met Steve in the seventh grade, that we would talk about such a project one day? Seriously, our teachers did not see that coming. I am grateful to Dr. Kendall Soulen for conversation on the meaning of the Atonement and his contributions to my writing on this topic. Some dear friends, who are colleagues in ministry and still kind enough to take my calls and questions after all these years, are more appreciated than they know. I am particularly grateful for the insights Mark Miller offered me about the nature of the Christian life.

The Ministry Resources team at Abingdon Press not only believed in this material enough to publish it; they also extended support and grace to the author during a crowded season of life. It means a lot when people offer you grace while you are writing a book on that topic. Ron Kidd's ability to simplify and organize material while editing made the book better.

Over the years that I have served as a pastor, people have told me about the joys and struggles of their lives. The honesty they shared when they discussed the messy aspects of their experience, along with the questions they carried about the Christian life, enabled me to understand both our need for Christ and his power to offer us hope. I am grateful for the trust they demonstrated when they shared those stories, as well as their desire to discover how faith in Christ could change their lives. It has been a great honor to be their pastor.

Most of all, I am grateful for the love of God that I have seen in all of our lives. We are so very fortunate that God is not through with any of us yet.

NOTES

Chapter 1

1. Paul Barolsky, "The Genius of Michelangelo's 'Creation of Adam' and the Blindness of Art History," in *Notes in the History of Art*, vol. 33, no. 1 (Fall 2013), 21-24, accessed August 24, 2016, http://www.jstor.org/stable/23595750.

2. Julie Miller, "Bill Murray Explains Why He Doesn't Have a Girlfriend," *Vanity Fair*, October 2014, accessed August 24, 2016, http://www.vanityfair.com/hollywood/2014/10/bill-murray -girlfriend.

Chapter 2

1. Martin Luther, quoted in Tullian Tchividjian, *Jesus + Nothing = Everything* (Wheaton, IL: Crossway, 2011), 39-40.

2. Jane E. Brody, "High Functioning, but Still Alcoholics," *New York Times*, May 4, 2009, accessed August 26, 2016, http://www.nytimes.com/2009/05/05/health/05brod.html?_r=0'.

3. Henri J. M. Nouwen, forward to H. Van Der Looy, *Rule for a New Brother* (Templegate Publishers, 1976), 8-9.

4. John Wesley, Sermon 85, "Working Out Our Own Salvation," Part II, 1, accessed August 26, 2016, http://wesley.nnu.edu/ john-wesley/the-sermons-of-john-wesley-1872-edition/sermon -85-on-working-out-our-own-salvation/.

5. Randy L. Maddox, *Responsible Grace: John Wesley's Practical Theology* (Nashville: Kingswood Books, 1994), 23.

6. Theodore Runyon, *The New Creation: John Wesley's Theology Today* (Nashville: Abingdon Press, 1998), 42.

7. Augustine, *Sermones de Scripturio Novi Testamenti*, CLXIX.xi.13, quoted in Runyon, *The New Creation*, 30.

Chapter 3

1. Richard J. Foster, "Salvation Is for Life," *Theology Today* 61 (2004), 298, accessed August 29, 2016, https://hopekaibear.files.wordpress .com/2008/05/salvationisforlife1.pdf.

2. Ibid., 299-300.

3. Elizabeth Leamy, "Stink Bugs Invade Homes, Are Called Menace to Agriculture," *Good Morning America–ABC News*, 3:25, April 15, 2011, http://abcnews.go.com/Business/ConsumerNews /stink-bugs-invade-homes-insect-pest-present-33/story?id =13379499.

4. Steven D. Levitt and Stephen J. Dubner, *Freakonomics: A Rogue Economist Explores the Hidden Side of Everything* (New York: HarperCollins, 2005), 21.

5. Ibid., 22.

6. Randy Maddox, *Responsible Grace*, 142.

7. Alcoholics Anonymous, 3rd edition (New York: Alcoholics Anonymous World Services, Inc., 1976), 59-60.

Chapter 4

1. "World's Top 19 Largest Crosses (Reach high for the Sky!)," *Miratico*, April 3, 2015, http://miratico.com/worlds-largest -crosses-reach-high-for-the-sky/.

2. *Frederick Hart, Sculptor*, ed. Paul Anbinder (New York: Hudson Hills Press, 1994), 76.

3. Alex Ayres, ed., *The Wit and Wisdom of Mark Twain* (New York: Harper and Row, 1987), 24.

Chapter 5

1. David McCullough Jr., "The 'You Are Not Special' Graduation Speech Is Just as Relevant Today," *Time*, November 17, 2015, http://time.com/4116019/david-mccullough-jr-graduation -speech-wellesley-high/.
2. Ibid.
3. D.P. Simpson, comp. *Cassell's New Compact Latin Dictionary*, s.v. "humilitas" and "humus." 1963. Reprint, New York: Dell Publishing Co., Inc., 1971.
4. Richard Foster, "Salvation Is for Life," 304.
5. Dallas Willard, *The Spirit of the Disciplines: Understanding How God Changes Lives* (New York: HarperCollins, 1991), 158.
6. Thomas G. Long, "Mary and Martha," *Day1*, published July 22, 2007, accessed September 1, 2016, http://day1.org/1052-mary _and_martha.

Chapter 6

1. Charles Wesley, "Love Divine, All Loves Excelling," *The United Methodist Hymnal* (Nashville: The United Methodist Publishing House, 1989), 384.